Women's Struggle for Equality

WOMEN'S STRUGGLE FOR EQUALITY

The First Phase, 1828–1876

Jean V. Matthews

The American Ways Series

IVAN R. DEE   *Chicago*

Library of Congress Cataloging-in-Publication Data:
Matthews, Jean V., 1937–
    Women's struggle for equality : the first phase. 1828–1876 / Jean
    V. Matthews.
        p.   cm. — (The American ways series)
    Includes bibliographical references and index.
        ISBN 1-56663-145-9 (alk. paper). —ISBN 1-56663-146-7 (pbk. :
alk. paper)
        1. Women's rights—United States—History. 2. Feminism—
United States—History.   I. Title.
HQ1236.5.U6M3845   1997
305.42'0973—dc21   96-47500

Contents

women in the movement. Question of racism, quarrels with old allies, and a split in the women's movement. NWSA and AWSA. What the split meant.

Preface

THE WOMEN'S MOVEMENT was one of the most important social and political forces of the nineteenth century. It was international in scope and, in its implications, profoundly
revolutionary. Its aim was to overturn the age-old and apparently universal "natural" and divinely ordained subordinate
position of women, claiming instead equality of rights, opportunities, and respect with men. Although the American movement made getting the vote an important goal from the
beginning, it was always concerned with women's emancipation in a much larger sense. Access to higher education and
the professions, and to wider fields of well-paid work; more
equal legal rights in marriage; control over their own bodies;
and perhaps, above all, a psychic transformation in women's
own estimation of themselves, their abilities, and their potential, were all important to nineteenth-century feminists.*
Until the latter half of the century, the vote was important
mainly as a potent symbol of the total transformation in
woman's position that was the feminists' primary aim, rather
than for any practical gains it might bring.

Modern feminists refer to the entire women's movement of
the nineteenth century, up to the achievement of the vote in
1920, as "first-wave feminism." But it would be more accurate

---

*Nineteenth-century people spoke of the woman movement, or the
woman's rights movement; the terms "feminist" and "feminism" were
not used until the early twentieth century, but I have employed them
from time to time in this book as a convenient, recognizable shorthand
for ideas and goals aiming at equality and self-development.

to apply that title only to the earlier years of the women's movement, through the 1870s. In many ways, in its origins, individualism, hostility to tight organization, dedication to self-discovery and "consciousness raising"; in its concern for issues of health and wrenching divisions on questions of sexuality; in a newly released rage, coupled with an often euphoric sense of a new world opening up to them, the early-nineteenth-century movement seems more the direct ancestor of the women's movement of the 1960s and 1970s than of the disciplined organizations that triumphed with the Nineteenth Amendment that provided for woman suffrage.

A veritable explosion of writing on women's history has occurred since Eleanor Flexner's pioneering account of the women's movement, *Century of Struggle*, appeared in 1959. Many of the major figures have received new biographies, the nineteenth-century women's press has been studied, and major collections of manuscripts have been made more widely accessible on microfilm. The antebellum period in particular has attracted scholarly attention, and we now know a good deal about women's lives and activities before the Civil War. This book builds upon this sizable body of work.

With notable exceptions such as Ellen Dubois and Mary Ryan, most historians of women after Eleanor Flexner have paid comparatively more attention to the social history of American women—to domesticity and prescriptive writing on womanhood, to working women, and to the social reform activities of middle-class women—than to the feminist movement, presumably on the assumption of its marginality to the lives of "average" women.

Certainly the women's movement involved only a very small minority of unusual women. Throughout most of the nineteenth century the mass of women were either indifferent or downright hostile to the agitation of "women's rights." Yet,

as with abolitionists of the 1830s or student radicals of the
1960s, the importance of the feminist pioneers was greater
than their numbers. They kept alive a vision not just of "improvement" in the condition of women but of transformation,
not just of reform but of equality. The existence of a women's
rights movement, even "Woman's Rights" as a slogan, represented possibilities whose power was magnified by the reaction of its many enemies, none of whom thought the
movement was less dangerous because of the small numbers
of self-proclaimed feminists.

The organized women's movement did not create the public problem of woman's role in the modern world. Rather it
emerged from the quite intense debate over the proper role
for women in modern democratic societies that had been present from the late eighteenth century. It was led by women
who were prepared to translate individual intellectual speculation into concrete demands and to organize women, however loosely, to agitate for their own emancipation. Few of the
concrete changes in the situation of women in the years from
1828 to 1876—more opportunities for higher education, reforms in the legal position of married women, more job opportunities for women—can be attributed mainly, or even at
all, to the agitation for women's rights. In some ways the
movement itself was stimulated by the beginnings of these
changes. Feminism was the way in which some women responded to, and hoped to shape, the rising expectations and
opportunities of nineteenth-century American life.

In refusing to accept the mystifications that masked the
costs of domestic subordination, and in probing the psychological as well as material damage done by restrictions that
hedged women in, the early feminists produced quite a penetrating critique of the gender arrangements of nineteenth-
century civilization. Through sheer dogged persistence, they

managed to build and sustain a movement that lasted seventy-two years, in itself an extraordinary achievement. Its existence, and the women who took part in it, were themselves exemplars both of the possibilities for self-emancipation and the ability of women to cooperate—though admittedly not without schisms—for long-term goals.

I wish to thank the University of Western Ontario for the sabbatical leave during which this book was written; the W. D. Weldon Library at Western, and particularly collections librarian Dave Newman; the Arthur M. and Elizabeth B. Schlesinger Library at Radcliffe for their help and hospitality during an extensive period of research; Widener Library at Harvard; and the libraries of the University of California at San Diego and San Diego State University for extending library privileges to me. I should also like to thank series editor John Braeman and Ivan Dee for editorial suggestions.

J. V. M.

Oakland, California
January 1997

Women's Struggle for Equality

1

The Woman Question

We too are primary existences.—Emma Willard, 1819

THE FIRST ORGANIZED and self-proclaimed movement for women's rights began with a convention of some
hundred women and men at Seneca Falls, New York, on July
19, 1848. The meeting was greeted with immediate conster-
nation and ridicule in much of the press as an astounding
attack on "the order of things established at the creation of
mankind." Yet the question of the "place," role, even the
"rights" of women had been the subject of considerable public
and private discussion since the end of the eighteenth century.
A growing amount of public print was taken up with arguments about the "nature" of woman; on whether, or how,
young ladies should be educated beyond common literacy;
on the relations of husbands and wives; on the duties and
power of motherhood; on the behavior patterns required of
a "lady"—a status now available to all broadly middle-class
women; on the responsibilities of women to the home; on the
economic problem of women unfortunate enough to have to
earn their own living; on the absolute necessity of young
women maintaining sexual purity and "delicacy"—and the

awful result when they did not. All these areas constituted what nineteenth-century people on both sides of the Atlantic called the "Woman Question." The agitation for women's rights represented the radical strand in this ongoing debate.

By the close of the eighteenth century the critical thinking of the Enlightenment and the ideology of liberty and equality that accompanied the American and French revolutions had called into question many kinds of traditional subordination. Even so, deeply rooted assumptions about racial inequality were barely touched, and the position of women scarcely at all. A few men in Europe and America had pondered how the role of women might be changed in the modern world; a few women had publicly demanded that the revolutionary values of equal rights be applied to them. But these were lone prophetic voices with little immediate effect.

Englishwoman Mary Wollstonecraft had issued a bold call for applying the rights of man to women, and her *Vindication of the Rights of Women* of 1792 was initially widely read in England and America. By the time of her early death in 1797, however, a reaction had set in. The excesses of the French Revolution had frightened many people out of experimenting with advanced ideas. From 1800 through the 1830s the United States was swept by a series of great religious revivals that profoundly affected the cultural tone of the country. There was to be a much stronger emphasis on strict sexual mores among respectable people and on the sanctity of marriage. When Wollstonecraft was revealed to have borne a child out of wedlock, public opinion considered her ideas irrevocably tainted, no longer suitable for open discussion by virtuous women. Yet her book continued to enjoy an underground existence (Lucretia Mott, a later leader of the women's rights movement, called it her "pet book"), and when in 1881 feminist leaders published a history of their movement, Wollstonecraft was among the "foremothers" to whom they dedicated it.

Still, by the early nineteenth century, in a republican and increasingly democratic political order, the traditional subordination of women, based on the assumption of their physical, mental, and moral inferiority to men, could no longer be taken for granted. Women's role had become sufficiently problematic that their subordination now had to be explicitly argued and their "place" more carefully delineated. In the process there was much shifting of position and many concessions. Complete equality of "rights" represented a "path not taken," but by the early nineteenth century a new set of assumptions about women's nature and role was evolving that offered them more room for maneuver and certainly enhanced their self-esteem. Insistence on women's inferiority became less blunt; subordination could be justified more kindly by emphasizing women's "difference" from men. The post-revolutionary sexual settlement hinged on this "difference" and the distinct social role and function it was taken to imply.

In the phrase that became one of the most constantly reiterated clichés of the nineteenth century, men and women were designed by God and nature to inhabit "separate spheres." Men were physically and mentally strong and courageous, and were thus meant for the rough and challenging world of war, work, and politics, as well as the professions and all the "higher" and more demanding realms of intellect and art. Women, physically and mentally weaker but morally purer, and with loving hearts and naturally self-sacrificing natures, were made for the home: for marriage, motherhood, domestic joys and charities. In short, men's sphere was the public world, women's the private.

The emphasis on a separate but dependent domestic sphere reflected the most basic fact of most women's lives in the nine-

teenth century. The overwhelming majority of American
women married, and once married, very few worked outside
the home for pay or had *independent* means of economic sub-
sistence, however productive their work within the household. Only a narrow range of ways was open for single
women or widows to earn money, and wage-earning women
always earned much less than men. For a woman, it was assumed, economic independence was a temporary and rather
unfortunate expedient, to be remedied when she could take
up her true vocation as wife and mother, supported by a husband. At the same time, as the urban and commercial-indus-
trial economy mushroomed in the first part of the nineteenth
century, especially in the Northeast, production was drawn
out of the household, and men's work increasingly took place
in offices, workshops, and factories separated from the home.
The husband's diminishing physical presence enhanced the
potential power and authority of the wife over domestic life,
and gave color to the idea that home was woman's "realm"
over which she presided like a queen.

A recognition of woman's authority *within her sphere* was
particularly noticeable in child-rearing. Nineteenth-century
writing on the proper bringing-up of children (a publishing
growth industry!) was now directed to mothers rather than to
fathers. Mothers were continually told how powerful was
their influence for good or ill over their children, and how
weighty was their consequent responsibility for the character
of the coming generation, and thus indirectly for the well-
being of the country. Indeed, "influence" over husbands and
children was the silent and invisible medium through which
the homebound woman was to put her impress upon the outside world. She was to live both *for* others and *through* them.

Historians have pointed out that we cannot take the idea of
separate spheres as a photographic image of the realities of

men's and women's lives in the nineteenth century. It was never applied to women in slavery and was limited even among free women. Very poor women could not sustain the withdrawn and comfortable home life demanded by the ideal of domesticity. And many middle-class women played a role in public life through charitable work or even reform causes. Even so, as an ideology the notion of separate spheres had tremendous power and influence. Public discourse on the Woman Question throughout the century is saturated with references to separate spheres. Nor was it only a middle-class ideology; the same insistence on role separation can be found among the skilled artisan class. Between 1830 and 1840 the number of magazine articles discussing and defining "woman's proper sphere" increased fourfold over the preceding decade—a sure indication of the ideological and promotional character of the concept.

The power and longevity of "separate spheres" derived from its usefulness and flexibility. Essentially it was a kind of sexual constitutionalism, a separation of powers designed to avoid competition and conflict between the sexes while affirming and molding gender identity. Theoretically it offered women a protected space of their own; while from the male point of view, like the "ladies auxiliaries" to fraternal societies, it deflected women from trying to invade male turf. The French writer Alexis de Tocqueville, who toured the United States in the early 1830s, praised the new nation for having hit on such a felicitous solution to the problem of the relation of the sexes in a democracy. "In no country," he remarked admiringly, "has such constant care been taken, as in America, to trace two clearly distinct lines of action for the two sexes." A rhetoric of "separate but equal," however, glossed over two fundamental assumptions in the doctrine of separate spheres—though they might be invoked only when some hardy woman tried to overstep the bounds: it was the nature of women to be always *dependent* on men, and women must never be put in a position where they would have authority over men—at least not men of their own class.

The policing of boundaries was an essential component in maintaining this gender constitution. In the early part of the century, clergy of the major denominations were particularly active in this regard; after the Civil War the medical profession came to the fore, and by the twentieth century, psychologists. Women were as active as men in this task of boundary maintenance. Formally, in the large numbers of advice books written by women for women, or in women's magazines and women's fiction, and informally, through gossip and social pressure, large numbers of women acted to keep potentially rebellious sisters in line and round up stragglers who seemed likely to venture outside the sphere or transgress its rules of propriety.

But the boundaries of the spheres were quite elastic. Much of women's history in the nineteenth century has been told as the story of the continuous efforts of middle-class women to extend the boundaries of their sphere without directly challenging the belief that there *was* a properly separate arena of female action. The essential point was not the precise content of the spheres, but agreement that there should be *some accepted boundary* delimiting the activities of men and women. Most men and women clung tenaciously to the idea of boundaries, even while the consensus on the content of woman's sphere was always subject to renegotiation. Thus in the first half of the century there were numerous instances of women expanding their options and activities in ways that fueled the debate on the Woman Question and formed much of the ferment from which feminism arose. What distinguished the advocates of women's rights was their insistence on equality, their free employment of a language of rights, and their repudiation of the very idea of boundaries.

While separate spheres was clearly the approach to the position of women in a modern democratic, Christian, capitalist order, preferred by most respectable people, an older tradition of rationalist Enlightenment radicalism had not been entirely submerged and remained as a thin but persistent stream in American life. Small groups of radicals who called themselves "Freethinkers" deplored the growing power of evangelical religion in American society. Others drawn to a new utopian socialism denounced the competitiveness and inequality of the incipient capitalist order. All were critical of traditional forms of marriage and the domestic seclusion of women. Among the most dynamic of such critics in the late 1820s were two British-born radicals based in New York, Frances Wright and Robert Dale Owen, son of the utopian socialist Robert Owen. In 1828 they founded a newspaper, the *Free Enquirer*, in which they argued for liberalization of divorce laws, birth control, the rights of working people, and the general rights of women.

Orphaned at an early age, Frances Wright inherited a good deal of money and thus was able to pursue an independent life that few other women of her age could even contemplate. At twenty-three she and her sister visited America and became converts to the socialist ideas of Robert Owen. In 1825 Wright used some of her wealth to set up an experimental community, Nashoba, in Tennessee with a few sympathetic whites and a number of slaves she purchased. Among other things, Nashoba was to be a model for the gradual abolition of slavery. The experiment soon foundered on economic mismanagement and sexual scandal, when it became public knowledge that this prototype for a new world included sex without marriage and, even more horrifying to most Americans, sexual relations between blacks and whites. In 1829 Wright wound down the settlement and freed her slaves in Haiti. She had already turned all her energies to extensive public lecturing in Eastern and Midwestern cities, championing universal free education as the key to real equality for all classes and both sexes and denouncing the clergy as enemies of freedom of thought. She wanted, she wrote, "to open the eyes" of women "to the nature of their situation in society." The key to women's inferior position, she insisted, was their ignorance and undeveloped intellects; the only remedy was an education equal to men's. She rested women's right to education squarely on the identical humanity of men and women. "In a daughter," she pointed out in one of her lectures, parents "have in charge a human being; in a son, the same. Let them train up these *human beings*, under the expanded wings of liberty" to the full development of all their faculties without distinction of sex or regard to future social roles.

As a lecturer, the tall, self-confident Wright was an immediate sensation and attracted large audiences. But she was savagely, even hysterically, denounced in the press and pulpits. Her attack on the churches was particularly shocking because it came from a woman. It was a commonplace of the time that women were not only naturally more religious than men but that religion was chiefly responsible for the "elevation" of woman in the modern world. Wright assaulted that connection by insisting that women were the dupes of religion rather than its beneficiaries. She had also provided ammunition for her attackers by defending in print the Nashoba experiment and its unconventional sexual arrangements. Conventional marriage laws were not in force at Nashoba, she wrote boldly, and this meant that "no woman can forfeit her individual rights or independent existence, and no man assert over her any rights or power whatsoever beyond what he may exercise over her free and voluntary affection."

The attacks on Frances Wright were due as much to the mere fact of her lecturing as to the matter of what she said. Wright was, in fact, the first woman ever to speak publicly in America before an audience of both men and women, thus breaking one of the major barriers between public and private spheres. She had "leaped over the boundary of feminine modesty, and laid hold upon the avocations of man," declared one newspaper; she had violated "the unalterable laws of nature." The clergy flung epithets such as "Whore of Babylon," "High Priestess of Belzebub," "The Red Harlot of Infidelity." The nickname "Fanny Wrighter" was for a long time a term of opprobrium applied to anyone venturing to challenge the doctrine of separate spheres.

Wright's time in the spotlight was short-lived. In 1830 she moved to France, married, and bore a daughter. By the time the family returned to America in 1835, the *Free Enquirer* had collapsed and the Hall of Science, where Wright had delivered her radical lectures, had become a Methodist church. Although Wright returned to lecturing and writing, she was never able to recapture her earlier successes or even her old notoriety. Increasingly estranged from both her husband and her daughter, when she died in Cincinnati in 1852 at the age of fifty-seven she was alone and largely forgotten.

Robert Dale Owen, Wright's friend and collaborator, did not suffer the same eclipse. In 1831 he published a book on the question that he and Wright had touched on in the *Free Enquirer*—birth control. This was a subject vital to women's future, but it was a question that most people, especially most women, thought to be far too delicate to deal with openly in public. In *Moral Physiology* Owen not only insisted, as later feminists would, that the final decision to have a child should be the wife's, but provided concrete information on how conception could be prevented. Like other men who dealt with the question at this time, Owen saw birth control primarily as a question of women's rights. "The whole life of an intellectual, cultivated woman," he wrote, should not be "spent in bearing a family of twelve or fifteen children."

When Dale Owen married in 1832, the bride's promise to obey was omitted, and he issued a public statement repudiating the powers that the law gave him over the property and person of his new wife. By the late 1830s Dale Owen had become sufficiently respectable to be elected to the legislature of Indiana, where he had settled. He tended to look back on his youthful radicalism as youthful folly, but he remained sufficiently true to his early commitment to women's rights to champion legislation on the property rights of married women and the liberalization of divorce laws.

Frances Wright had lectured with a copy of the Declaration of Independence in her hand as a reminder to Americans of their revolutionary heritage of natural rights. This same heritage fueled an incipient feminism among some of America's earliest industrial workers, the young women who were the bulk of the work force in the early textile mills of New England. They were mainly girls from hard-pressed New England farms, native-born, Protestant, and literate. There was a sprinkling of clearly middle-class women, daughters of ministers or craftsmen who had fallen on hard times. Young and single, except for the occasional older widow, they lived in company-run boardinghouses in mill villages. Living away from home in this all-female atmosphere produced a sense of independence and solidarity. Their work was hard, but compared to other women workers they were well paid, and they valued the money and the independence it brought. At the same time they knew they were not permanent workers; they were in the mills for two or three years until they married. They did not think of themselves as "working class"; they acknowledged, with a mixture of defensiveness and pride, that they were "working girls," but they were also "daughters of freemen," whose grandfathers had fought in the Revolution.

This self-confidence came out very clearly in one of the first strikes, in Lowell in 1834, to protest a wage cut. About eight hundred girls turned out and, as reported by the local newspaper, "one of the leaders mounted a stump and made a flaming Mary Wollstonecraft speech on the rights of women and the iniquities of the *'monied* aristocracy.'" To the male reporter, the mere sight of a young woman making a speech in the open air denouncing employers was evidence of a claim to "women's rights." A similar (and similarly unsuccessful) strike in 1836 produced the same rhetoric of resistance to tyranny and a claim to the Revolutionary heritage.

By the 1840s resistance among the mill workers had turned from direct action to agitation for legislative enactment of a ten-hour working day. Lowell women banded together in a Female Labor Reform Association and joined with the New England Workingmen's Reform Association to petition the Massachusetts legislature. Though a group of mill women testified personally before a legislative investigating committee, the legislature refused to act, and by 1848 the Reform Association had fallen apart. By the 1850s the Ten Hour Movement was largely a movement of workingmen, not women.

During the brief existence of the Female Labor Reform Association, its newspaper, *The Voice of Industry*, and other New England labor papers, had been filled with articles and letters from working women employing a language of rights, not only as workers but as women. They denounced the assumed superiority of men, asserting women's right to education and to work in whatever kind of job their strength and intelligence was equal to. They denied the common assumption that men "protected" women and demanded: "treat us as equals . . . restore to us our rights." A writer who signed herself only as "An Indignant Factory Girl" excoriated marriage as a relation where woman had "lost her individuality," and exhorted: "Away with the base admission of the old lie of inferiority; away with submitting and servility."

In spite of an evident feminist consciousness among some of these factory girls, they did not as *a group* become a component of the soon-to-be launched women's movement. By the 1850s, indeed, the composition of the New England mill labor force was changing rapidly as single girls were replaced by largely immigrant families. This constituency could certainly produce labor militancy, but it was not fertile ground for feminism. Young women who lived at home with their immigrant parents were less impressed with the language of individual rights. Yankee mill girls married or turned to other kinds of jobs in which they were more scattered. They had less opportunity to develop a group sense of rights as women. For the rest of the century the women's movement never found a constituency of such potential among wage-earning women as the mill girls had seemed for a brief moment to be.

Within limits the doctrine of women's sphere, while rigorously avoiding assertion of rights or equality, was sufficiently expansive to allow women to make certain practical gains. This was particularly true in the area of education. Frances Wright had linked better education for women to *equality* and situated it in a discourse of natural rights. But female education could be more comfortably and more successfully promoted as necessary to make women more intelligent "modern" wives and mothers. From the 1820s onward there was a marked increase of interest in offering middle-class girls a more serious education than the smattering of "accomplishments" hitherto available to a few upper-class young women.

A momentous development for the history of women in the early nineteenth century was the progress of female literacy. Where it had previously lagged far behind men's, it now began to draw closer. Historians estimate that by 1850, half of American women were literate, a figure that obscures great regional and racial disparities. In the increasingly urbanized and commercial Northeast, both male and female literacy among whites approached 97 percent. Free African-Americans were often barred from public schools in the Northern states; even so, in Pennsylvania, which held the largest free black population, about half of African-American women were literate by 1850. Growing literacy was accompanied by a huge increase in the amount and availability of reading matter. The number of newspapers, magazines, and novels grew remarkably in the first half of the nineteenth century, making available to more and more people an expanding intellectual world of the imagination and of information beyond the small society of face-to-face contacts.

Literacy could be acquired in a myriad of informal ways, but by the early nineteenth century the common schools in New England were open to girls, and coeducation at this basic level soon became the accepted norm wherever elementary school systems were established. Education at a higher level was a different matter. No colleges admitted women; a few girls with strong minds and liberal parents might receive a good education from fathers or tutors, but generally the idea of the "learned female" or "bluestocking" was a subject of ridicule. Yet there was clearly a yearning among many women for the opportunity to expand their minds. Even women who did not challenge the general subordination of women to men often found the assumption that women were by nature less intelligent especially humiliating. Middle-class young women with college-educated brothers in particular were often miserably aware that the siblings with whom they had played as equals were now moving away from them into a world of mental expansion and opportunities from which they were shut out. Women were always prominent in audiences for the public lectures given in most American towns from the 1830s on, on subjects of general cultural interest from the latest discoveries in chemistry to Shakespeare's plays. Aspiring women came together in numerous study clubs and reading groups, like the "Improvement Circle" set up by a group of mill girls at Lowell, or the African-American Female Literary Association of Philadelphia, or the Edgeworthalean Society in Bloomington, Indiana, designed to stimulate "mental and moral culture."

Two successful pioneers in opening higher education opportunities to women, Emma Willard and Catharine Beecher, both felt keenly the deprivation of educational opportunities, and refused to acknowledge that women were *mentally* inferior to men. But they couched much of their propaganda in terms of the duties of mothers, placing their arguments in the context of the different nature and future roles of the two sexes. Nor did they propose to batter down the doors of the established men's colleges; rather, they took the "separate spheres" route of creating special new institutions for girls alone, halfway between high school and college.

Willard opened a "female academy" in the new town of Troy, New York, in 1821, designed to give upper- and middle-class young women as solid an academic education as their brothers received in college. Between 1821 and 1872 Willard's school educated some twelve thousand girls—among them the young Elizabeth Cady, who became one of the leaders of the later women's rights movement. Many of Willard's scholars became teachers for at least a portion of their lives and, with the geographical mobility so characteristic of nineteenth-century Americans, spread what the historian Anne Firor Scott has called "the widening circle" of Willard's influence over much of the eastern United States.

Willard's commitment to improved education for women was based squarely on the conviction that, in her words, "we too are primary existences." Even so, she also remained convinced that women's general subordination to men was part of the divine plan. So did the even more famous and influential proponent of women's education, Catharine Beecher, eldest daughter of one of America's most important evangelical ministers. Convinced that "there is in mind no distinction of sex," she opened the Hartford Female Seminary in 1823, determined to provide solid education and to graduate women who would use their trained minds in their "natural" vocation as teachers—either as mothers in their own homes, or before, or even instead of, marriage as professional teachers. Soon leaving the seminary to be run by others, Beecher launched a career as a prolific writer, publicist, and fund-raiser for the cause of teacher training for women.

Willard and Beecher were both horrified by Frances Wright and quick to dissociate themselves and their projects for improving female education from her advocacy of that cause. Willard denounced her for seeking to "break the link which God has instituted and in which woman, in obedience to her nature and express commands of God, acknowledges man as her head." Catharine Beecher was as much distressed by Wright as an exemplar of what women could become as by her ideas, and denounced her "great masculine person, her loud voice, her untasteful attire." Particularly disturbing to

Beecher was the fact that Wright traveled about "unprotected . . . feeling no need of protection, mingling with men in stormy debate."

Like Willard, Catharine Beecher had a strong psychological investment in the ideology of separate spheres. Both women became prominent opponents of the later women's rights movement, and objected to any suggestion that women should vote or attempt to break into "male" professions such as the law. Beecher was one of the first in a long line of women who have attempted to raise the status and self-esteem of women by reevaluating their traditional domestic work and insisting it be regarded as a "profession," parallel but not inferior to male professions. Her most popular book, the 1841 *Treatise on Domestic Economy*, and its 1869 enlargement, *The American Woman's Home*, addressed women as intelligent and competent managers. These works provided not just recipes and household hints but information and instruction on child-rearing, home nursing, hygiene, and even designs for healthy and convenient houses. If it were approached in a scientific spirit, Beecher was convinced that homemaking would provide all necessary scope for the educated woman to use her intellect. "No American woman," she insisted, "has any occasion for feeling that hers is an humble or insignificant lot."

The cause of female education tied to piety, service, and acceptance of a dignified separate sphere enjoyed considerable success. By the 1850s there were numerous female academies throughout the country, including the Southern states, with varying degrees of academic rigor. More than thirty chartered institutions called themselves female *colleges* and granted degrees. Only a few were open to free African-American girls, but the desire for education was strong, and a few young women from the small free black middle class did manage to gain access to some higher education. In the 1830s African-

American Sarah Maps Douglas of Philadelphia founded the first institution offering a high school education to black girls.

None of these academies had any overt intention of challenging the separate, and subordinate, sphere of women. All constantly reiterated that the primary aim of female education was to make girls better "daughters, wives and mothers." The historian Keith Melder has gone so far as to call these institutions "masks of oppression," seeing them as educating for conformity rather than liberation. They certainly seem to have been delivering mixed messages. One young graduate of Hartford Seminary insisted to a friend that "mental acquirements" were quite compatible with "the domestic usefulness of a woman." Even so, she added, "I think however great the acquirements which a woman has made, they should never be blazoned to the world—should be kept in the shade and never exhibited or displayed."

Even the few instances of coeducation at the college level during these years were not undertaken with radical intent. Oberlin College in Ohio, opened in 1837, was the first college in America to admit women as well as men—and indeed, blacks as well as whites. Dedicated to the spread of Christian perfectionism, Oberlin's assumption was always that the female graduate would exert her educated moral influence through the home. Though the college was coeducational, a separate "Ladies Course" omitted the classical languages, mathematics, and theology. Women students who insisted were allowed to take the regular degree course. Among those who did was twenty-five-year-old Lucy Stone, who had spent seven years in various teaching jobs to save enough money for college. Already committed to a belief in real equality for women, she soon found herself at odds with the faculty's conventional notions of female propriety and woman's sphere. She graduated with honors but refused to write an essay for the graduation ceremony because as a woman she would not have been allowed to deliver it herself but would have had to listen to a man read it for her.

Still, the experience of education made tangible changes in young women's lives. A study of Mount Holyoke Seminary, founded in 1837, reveals that its graduates tended to marry somewhat later than most American women, which meant that their characters were more fully formed by the time they settled down to domestic life. They also had smaller families than their contemporaries (a pattern also characteristic of the early New England mill girls). Moreover, the belief that "mind has no sex" had enormous liberating potential. Oberlin and the best of the academies, for all their timidities, took young women's minds seriously and offered a quite wide exposure to literature, philosophy, and science as well as to large doses of domestic propaganda. Though many girls were enrolled in these schools for only a term or two, for that brief period they were individuals entitled to self-development rather than daughters, wives, or mothers devoted to the needs of others. It was an experience that could raise heady ambitions. "I want to be prepared for any station," confided one young Mount Holyoke student to her diary. "I must rise & *be nothing no longer*." In the academies too, many of the teachers and even the principals were women and thus provided a model of women in authority. Elizabeth Cady Stanton was not particularly impressed by her years at Troy, but she remembered Emma Willard as a woman with "profound self-respect (a rare quality in a woman) which gave her a dignity truly regal."

The growth of women's educational opportunities also enabled many young women to take advantage of the great expansion of public schooling in the North and West to earn a measure of financial independence as teachers. Since the pub-

lic wanted schools but did not wish to pay very much for
them, the demand for teachers soon outran the supply of men
who were willing to take these jobs. Young women, however,
who had so few alternatives for "respectable" work outside
the home, would teach school for a few years before marriage
for a third to a half of what a man would be paid. True, most
women teachers served for only a brief period and at low
salaries, but the experience offered a taste of independence,
self-support, and even authority. The historian Joan Jensen, in
a study of teaching in Pennsylvania, insists that teaching provided "an essential transition . . . from a functional to a liberating literacy through which [women] could interact with the
social and intellectual life of the new nation in ways that only
males had done earlier."

The closing of the literacy gap between men and women,
and the availability of at least some education for some
women beyond the elementary, were important developments
for women. It seems unlikely that a feminist movement could
have arisen without the achievement of a high degree of female literacy and the access that many women were gaining to
a wider education. Even so, while education heightens the
sense of self, imparts greater self-confidence, and extends the
range of imaginable possibilities, it does not automatically
transform young women into advocates of women's rights.
Almost all the women's rights leaders of the nineteenth century had had a better formal education than most of their contemporaries. But the same can be said for the most prominent
and articulate of women *opposed* to the women's rights movement, such as Catharine Beecher. Education enabled women
to think more consciously about what it meant, or should
mean, to be a woman, and to participate articulately in public
discussion of the Woman Question—but it did not determine
what position they would take in this debate.

One major consequence of the widening of the female reading public together with the expansion of the publishing industry was a notable increase in the number of publications directed specifically at women, and the number of women who themselves broke into print. By the 1850s women writers dominated the fiction market. A few women were able to earn quite a respectable living from their pen, and many women who would never become professional authors managed to publish something in struggling magazines desperate for contributions. Whatever the literary merit of these works, their success and visibility was an important boost for women's consciousness. Women were also becoming magazine editors. The most famous was Sarah Josepha Hale, who from 1837 to 1877 edited *Godey's Ladies Book*, the largest-circulation magazine of the first half of the century, with 150,000 subscribers in 1860 and a readership many times that. Widowed at thirty-four, with five young children, Hale had turned to writing as a way to earn money while taking care of her young family, and from that moved on to magazines. Throughout her long and successful career she always defended domestic life as the proper sphere for women; her own departure from domesticity was the result of misfortune, not choice.

But like Catharine Beecher, Hale was a complex figure. A staunch supporter of woman's separate sphere, she opposed any agitation for women's rights or female involvement in politics. "The term *rights of woman*," she editorialized in 1833, "is one to which I have an almost constitutional aversion." But she also firmly insisted on "the equal dignity" of her sex and its equal, if perhaps different, intellectual ability, and she was a tireless promoter of women's schools. From her own experience she knew that it was not an ideal world and that women could not always count on comfortable homes supported by a male wage. In her columns she endorsed a surprisingly wide range of income-producing work that she thought suitable for women—including medicine. Like Catharine Beecher, Hale believed that homemaking required skill and training (she is credited with coining the term "domestic science"); above all, like Beecher, she was a promoter of women's self-esteem and women's interests as she saw them.

Publication is a claim to public authority. For this reason, as Mary Kelley has shown, women authors in this period often seemed quite uncomfortable with their role. Most women writers and the majority of articles in women's magazines adhered to the doctrine of separate spheres. But however conventional the author's overt message, the author herself was an example of a woman acting in the public realm, and earning money by doing so. Women as editors or popular writers, like women as teachers or school principals, offered living exemplars that were often at odds with the ideology they professed and used their position to convey. As the feminist Lucretia Mott commented of Sarah Hale, she "in theory believed in the entire subordination of women to the other sex; but her practice was somewhat the reverse, and no one acted more independently than she."

Some historians have described women like Hale and Beecher as "domestic feminists," moving toward feminist goals by rather different means than the women's rights advocates. But this is to ignore their own frequent and strong antifeminist statements. They shared with the articulate feminist movement that developed after 1848 a concern for certain practical intermediate goals, such as better educational opportunities, the improvement of women's health, and more and better-paying jobs for women who were forced to earn their own living. They also took aim at many of the same targets: the women who ruined their health by their own lack of common sense, the expensive but superficial education in useless "accomplishments" offered by too many schools for girls, and the idle, foolish woman who was a slave to fashion (*Godey's Ladies Book* owed much of its popularity to its elaborate fashion plates, included by publisher Louis Godey over Hale's protests). Nonetheless they were operating from fundamentally different premises and had a quite different vision for women.

As the historian Frances B. Cogan has pointed out, in the mid-nineteenth century there were several patterns of womanhood competing for the allegiance of American women. The ideal promoted by women such as Hale, Beecher, and others, Cogan has dubbed "Real Womanhood," to distinguish it both from the excessively submissive and anemic version of women, often labeled by clergy and other moralists as "true women," and from the new radical model offered by the women's movement. The "Real Woman" of the Beecher/Hale persuasion was to be healthy, intelligent, vigorous, and thoroughly competent, but she would never abandon feminine "delicacy" or the acknowledgment of her ultimate dependence on men. Woman's sphere was to be preserved, expanded, and "elevated," but the barriers between it and men's sphere were to remain intact.

Many women were practically expanding women's sphere during this period by their growing activity outside the home in various kinds of volunteer benevolent and "social work." Women organizing with women in this sort of activity was one of the most striking developments of the antebellum period. A booming but unstable economy, rapid urbanization in the Northeast and Midwest, and great geographical mobility produced growing numbers of economic victims, most of them, then as now, women and children. The meager local government provisions for poor relief were overwhelmed, but the slack was taken up by new voluntary organizations, many of them composed entirely of women.

African-American women in Northern cities were among the earliest to organize mutual aid self-help societies to relieve impoverished black people who could expect little from civic institutions. Inspired by the great religious revivals of the early 1800s, many middle-class white women organized societies to distribute Bibles or food and fuel to widows and orphans, to run Sunday schools, to raise money to enable poor young men to train for the ministry, and even to found, finance, and run orphanages for parentless or abandoned children. Many of these societies were formed as an adjunct of a particular church, and in these the minister and the leading men of the congregation directed the activities of the women; but others were quite autonomous and were run entirely by the women themselves. By the 1850s there were thousands of such societies in cities and small towns across the nation, though there were far more—and they were more likely to be entirely run by women—in the North than in the South.

Many women joined the male-led Temperance movement against drunkenness, and by the 1830s most local Temperance groups were probably at least half female. The insistence of many male Temperance leaders that women's role in the movement be strictly subordinate, however, caused considerable tension, and by the early 1850s a few Temperance women were espousing women's rights. More radical both in tactics and ideology were the numerous "moral reform" societies that sprang up in the 1830s, particularly in Massachusetts and New York state, to combat the growing problem of prostitution. Outspoken in their denunciation of the "double standard" of sexual morality, the moral reformers were often led by their concern for the sexual vulnerability of young women to a consideration of the economic exploitation of women and the problems caused by their lack of economic independence. Some women who later became leaders of the women's rights movement had had an earlier involvement with moral reform: Susan B. Anthony, for example, and Lucretia Mott. But most of the moral reformers recoiled from an overt commitment to or advocacy of women's rights.

Some historians have traced the origins of the women's rights movement to a "transformation in the sense of self," which they attribute to the thousands of women in cities and small towns who associated to help other women. Other historians have drawn a sharp distinction between the kinds of women who worked for benevolent "welfare" associations and those involved in reform work, and between these and feminists. In her study of the booming commercial town of Rochester, New York, one of the great hotbeds of antebellum revivalism, female association, and reform, Nancy Hewitt found three separate networks of activist women, with little overlap: a charity relief network, an evangelical revivalist network aiming to rid society of intemperance and vice, and what Hewitt calls the "ultras"—a small but highly vocal and visible group of socially marginal women who championed all the radical reforms of the age, including racial and sexual equality. Separated by style, associates, religious affiliation, and objects of attention, the women of these different networks operated on different assumptions about the nature of woman and her proper role in the world. The fundamental dividing line, says Hewitt, was between the ultras and the other two groups. The latter were involved to varying degrees in expanding woman's sphere; the ultras were breaking down the boundaries.

Thus women's voluntary associations, like education, have an ambiguous relation to the growth of the women's rights movement. Women learned to organize and to administer institutions and even quite large sums of money. They learned to cooperate with other women outside the family, and probably in the process of all this acquired a higher esteem for themselves and for their sex. But in so far as woman's sphere became roomier throughout this period, providing scope for organizational skills, achievement, and status, many women felt less inclined to kick against its limits. Much female activism was in defense of woman's sphere, not an escape from it. Still, organizational womanhood may have been creating a new female type. "I think gentle, dependent women are 'out of Fashion,' as it were," remarked one young woman rather wistfully in 1854. "At least, people now-a-days seem to prefer *strong minded, decided, sensible* women."

2

Challenging Roles, Asserting Rights

Thus vaguely are these questions proposed and discussed at present. But their being proposed at all implies much thought and suggests more. Many women are considering within themselves, what they need that they have not, and what they can have, if they find they need it. Many men are considering whether women are capable of being and having more than they are and have, *and*, whether, if so, it will be best to consent to improvement in their condition.—Margaret Fuller, 1845

THE PIVOTAL REFORM of the years before the Civil War was the antislavery movement, and it provided the strongest bridge between female activism and feminism. In the early 1830s the muted antislavery feelings that had existed since the Revolution were galvanized into vibrant and controversial new life by the radical William Lloyd Garrison. Proclaiming slavery a sin and calling for immediate abolition, he had no qualms about appealing to women. By 1838 there were more than a hundred separate women's societies among the local auxiliaries to the American Anti-Slavery Society. The women raised funds for the cause and were an important source of financial support. In the face of harassment and insults, they launched major petition campaigns in 1837 and 1838, urging Congress to abolish slavery in Washington, D.C., and the territories.

While petitioning government was a legitimate political activity open to women, since the petition is a "request" from a subordinate to a superior, the subject on which they petitioned was an explosive one. Deluged with such petitions, Congress reacted with a "gag rule," in effect until 1844, essentially refusing to accept or read the petitions. One reason given was that so many had been signed by women, who had no business to concern themselves with matters of such national importance. As one congressman remarked, it was "exceedingly indelicate that sensitive females of shrinking modesty should present their names here as petitioners."

Both antislavery activity and the response to it thus raised the whole question of the extent to which women were citizens, morally obligated to concern themselves with political questions and entitled to lobby government about them. Women who had screwed up their courage to circulate or sign a petition now had a graphic example of how little influence they really had. All antislavery women, by their very involvement in this deeply unpopular cause, had already stepped over a line into something most people thought dangerous and improper. The opposition they encountered because of their sex caused some of them to begin to question their position as women. A key development was the brief meteoric career of the Grimké sisters.

Daughters of a prominent South Carolina slaveholding family, Sarah and Angelina Grimké had become dissatisfied with what seemed to them the vacuous life of the upper-class Southern girl. Sarah in particular resented the fact that the good advanced education given to her brothers was denied to her. In her late twenties she left home for Philadelphia and was later joined by the younger Angelina. The sisters became converts to Garrison's abolition crusade and in 1836 were recruited to become antislavery agents speaking to groups of women.

Angelina Grimké turned out to be an orator of considerable power. During her speaking tour a number of men began coming to hear her, so that she found herself lecturing to what the nineteenth century called "promiscuous audiences," that is, consisting of both men and women. For a woman to speak to audiences in which men were present reopened the public controversy that had swirled around Fanny Wright. In July 1837 the Ministerial Association of the Congregational Churches of Massachusetts issued a public "Pastoral Letter" clearly aimed at Grimké, making plain the church's position on the role of women. They appreciated, said the ministers, the "unostentatious prayers" of woman and her work in charities.

> But when she assumes the place and tone of man as a public reformer, our care and protection of her seem unnecessary; we put ourselves in self-defense against her. . . . If the vine, whose strength and beauty is to lean upon the trellis-work, and half conceal its clusters, thinks to assume the independence and overshadowing nature of the elm, it will not only cease to bear fruit, but fall in shame and dishonor into the dust.

This letter was read from every orthodox pulpit in New England and was taken as a stunning rebuke. To some women, however, it became a spur rather than a deterrent. When nineteen-year-old Lucy Stone heard it read in her church, she was furious and resolved that if she ever had anything to say in public, she "would say it, and all the more because of that pastoral letter."

It is difficult now to appreciate the commotion occasioned then by women speaking in public. Women's voices were in fact being heard more and more often on certain kinds of public occasions involving mixed audiences. Women were praying aloud at revival meetings; roving women preachers could be found on the evangelical fringes; and Quakers allowed women to preach. Even acting in the theater was becoming more respectable for women by the late 1830s.

Angelina Grimké was not even the first woman since Frances Wright to give public lectures to mixed-sex audiences. She had been preceded five years earlier by a free black, Maria Stewart of Boston. Aware that she was treading on dangerous ground, Stewart had invoked biblical precedents for her temerity in speaking, and situated herself as a modern descendant of biblical women in leadership roles. "What if I am a woman?" she demanded. "Is not the God of ancient times the God of these modern days? Did he not raise up Deborah to be a mother and a judge in Israel?" Stewart seems to have been accepted until she angrily denounced black men for what she saw as their frivolity and lack of spirit, at a time when the position of free people of color was worsening. At this point a storm of criticism from the African-American community drove her off the platform and out of the city.

These examples of women's public voices, however, were occasioned by extraordinary religious excitement, peripheral religious sects, or, in the case of the theater, a situation in which the speaker, however compelling, was "entertaining" rather than instructing the audience. Stewart had indeed spoken to instruct and reprove, and had offended some African Americans in doing so, but she had no impact on the white public. The Grimkés, on the other hand, were upper-class native-born white women; to white society their flouting of propriety was far more serious.

The public "oration" was one of the distinctive, and distinc-
tively masculine, aspects of early-nineteenth-century American culture. The public speaker was seen as a man of authority
and power, displaying *mastery* over his audience through his
logic, eloquence, and personality. Women such as Emma
Willard and Catharine Beecher, whenever they offered public
addresses, always made a point of remaining seated while
their speech was read for them by a man. Similarly, Dorothea
Dix, the tireless campaigner for better treatment of the insane
and probably the most effective single reformer of the antebellum period, addressed written memorials to state legislatures
but always had them presented for her by a male speaker.
These maneuvers now seem absurd, but these women were
making a fine distinction that was very important to them. To
stand at the lecturer's desk would have been to claim authority
and to forfeit a lady's modesty and delicacy.

In addition to the wrath of the clergy, Angelina Grimké
also incurred the displeasure of Catharine Beecher. In 1837
Beecher published an "Essay on Slavery and Abolitionism,
with Reference to the Duty of American Females," addressed
explicitly to Angelina. Beecher's biographer, Katheryn Kish
Sklar, says that she saw in Angelina Grimké one of her major
competitors "for the allegiance of a newly self-conscious generation of American women." Beecher deplored any female
involvement in anything so controversial as the antislavery
movement. Women who wished to do good in the world had
plenty of scope in the vital task of educating children. Grimké
replied with *Letters to Catharine Beecher* in 1838, filled with
what had by now become a fast-blossoming feminism. In the
same year her sister Sarah published *Essays on the Equality of
the Sexes*.

The sisters started from premises rather different from

those of Fanny Wright. Wright had assumed the fundamental equality of both sexes as human beings, and from that natural human equality flowed their equal "natural" rights. The Grimkés, who were devoutly if unorthodoxly religious, started from the equality of men and women as moral beings, with equal moral *duties* as children of God. But imperative duties implied the *right* to carry them out. If women had a moral duty to combat the great sin of the age, slavery, they had a right to do so in whatever way they found necessary. In a period when mainstream women were emphasizing their distinctiveness as a sex, the Grimkés played down such distinctions in order to point up the commonality of moral duty for men and women. The "mere circumstance of sex does not give to man higher rights and responsibilities, than to woman," Angelina insisted. "My doctrine then is, that whatever it is morally right for man to do, it is morally right for woman to do . . . for in Christ Jesus there is neither male nor female." This gospel equality took her a long way: by the end of the paragraph she was insisting that women had a *right* to a voice in all the laws by which they were governed in church or state, even a right to sit in Congress or be president.

To Sarah, men's assumption of superiority over women was not natural but usurped. It had resulted in multiple oppressions, from the unequal laws of marriage to the low wages of working women. Coupled with racial pride, it allowed the white man to subject his slave women to his lust without remorse. But the worst consequence was that women themselves internalized male belief in their inferiority. Among the upper classes, fashionable women were regarded by men, and by themselves, "as pretty toys or as mere instruments of pleasure." Among the vast middle class, the married woman was a domestic drudge. Taught to regard the routine of the house-

hold as "the end of her being," the housewife came to see herself only "as a kind of machinery, necessary to keep the domestic engine in order."

Women had been forced and cajoled to surrender rights in
return for privileges, and their moral nature had been cor-
rupted in the process. " 'Rule by obedience and by submission
sway,' or in other words, study to be a hypocrite," wrote Sarah
contemptuously. "Pretend to submit, but gain your point, has
been the code of household morality which woman has been
taught." "I ask no favors for my sex," was her essential message to men. "All I ask of our brethren is, that they take their
feet from off our necks, and permit us to stand upright on that
ground which God designed us to occupy." What is remark-
able in these writings is how quickly the Grimkés had articu-
lated a full-fledged feminist position, and their emphasis on
the psychological damage done to women by their subordinate
and dependent position.

The activities of the sisters aroused opposition within as
well as outside the abolitionist movement. Many feared that
the introduction of the woman question would turn people
away from the more important issue of antislavery. Theodore
Weld, one of the most outspoken of the antislavery orators,
and Angelina's mentor as a speaker, wrote to her in August
1837 suggesting that if she would just concentrate on *slavery*,
people would come round to accepting her public speaking;
but if she insisted on *proclaiming her right to do so* she would
create unnecessary antagonism. This attitude was shared by
some women. The abolitionist writer Lydia Maria Child, for
example, endorsed women acting boldly, but she shrank from
an explicit assertion of rights. Words, as both she and Weld
recognized, are often more provocative than actions.

Weld's hesitant letter was not well received by Angelina.
"The *time* to assert a right is *the* time when *that* right is de-

nied," she replied. This dispute seems to have stimulated their growing romantic feelings for each other, and in May 1838 Weld and Angelina were married. Like Dale Owen, Weld publicly renounced any "rights" over Angelina's property or person.

Angelina Grimké, now thirty-two, had not expected to marry. As she jokingly told Weld, men "stoutly declare that women who hold such sentiments of *equality* can never expect to be courted. They seem to hold out this as a kind of threat to deter us from asserting our rights." The couple retired to a small farm in New Jersey, taking Sarah with them. Here they led an austere life, and Angelina was gradually worn down by lack of money and household help, poor health, and three children. Both Theodore and Angelina sincerely wished to put marriage on a new, egalitarian footing, but they also believed it important to demonstrate to a skeptical world that a feminist woman could also be a "good" wife, mother, and homemaker, a domestic paragon. Friends who visited the rather bleak household were saddened by the eclipse of the sisters' talents. Angelina emerged to speak briefly at a women's rights convention in 1851 and again in 1863, but she was effectively lost to feminism as a major leader.

Nonetheless her example emboldened others. A young Quaker schoolteacher, Abby Kelley, by 1838 was also addressing mixed audiences and became one of the most famous antislavery orators. Unlike the Grimkés, she did not end her activities when she married a fellow abolitionist. While the spectacle of a woman addressing a public meeting could still arouse ridicule, catcalls, denunciations from the pulpit, and disapproval from the majority of conventional women, this particular barrier had now been cracked. By the late 1840s and 1850s more and more women were attempting the public platform. The questions raised by the Grimké sisters had come as a liberating revelation to at least some women in abolitionist circles. "Sarah's writings are doing wonders," wrote one woman. "Some few females have Emancipated themselves and are beginning to stand erect." After hearing Angelina speak, she added revealingly, "I have ever since been struggling into existence."

Renewed interest in the more radical aspects of the Woman Question spilled over into a wider public. In January 1838 the Boston Lyceum sponsored a public debate on the equality of the sexes. Both sides were defended by male speakers, and when the male members of the large audience were invited to vote, they decided against sexual equality. Even Boston schoolgirls were debating the Woman Question, including whether women should have the right to vote. Thirteen-year-old Ednah Dow Littlehale and her friend Caroline Healey got into a heated correspondence.

Both girls had romantic notions of making their mark in the world. But, declared Ednah dramatically in one letter, "we have the misfortune to be *women* . . . we must see ourselves *slaves*, Slaves to what? To *custom*, a *tyrant* worse than the most tyrannical king. . . . It is a crime for a *woman* to speak her thoughts." She closed with a rousing peroration: "*American Women.* . . . ye are denied all political rights, ye are subjected to your *tyrants men.* . . . Stand up and assert your rights, be *slaves* no longer." She thought women should refuse to get married until men were prepared to allow them their "full political rights."

Caroline replied loftily from the superiority of her fifteen years: "What mean you, by the political rights of women? . . . . would you wish your husband to stay at home and take care of your children? for you to go to Caucus? . . . . I think you are a *ninny* to call yourself a slave. I am not one." It was true, she conceded, "I thought just so at your age," but now she knew better: "I *wish* to be a perfect lady, however far short I may fall of the mark." Ednah was not to be intimidated: "I know what I am saying, I am equal to the men, and not superior to them. I am a slave until I am free, & I am not free yet. . . . If you don't think women have as good a right to vote as men you ought to be ducked in the *frog pond*." In spite of these differences, as grown-ups both girls joined the women's rights movement.

The injection of the woman question into abolitionism did not recede with the removal of the Grimké sisters. When in 1840 Garrison proposed Abby Kelley for the American Anti-Slavery Society business committee, a number of men resigned in protest and formed a rival antislavery society. That same year the Woman Question spilled over onto the international scene, at the World's Anti-Slavery Convention in London. Seven women were among the official delegates from the United States, including Lucretia Mott, the highly respected Quaker leader of Philadelphia's abolitionist women. The British hosts, however, refused to accept their credentials and seat them because of their sex. Their right to participate was defended by fellow delegates Wendell Phillips and Garrison, but to no avail. The women spent the convention as silent onlookers in the gallery.

Among them was the twenty-five-year-old Elizabeth Cady Stanton, the new bride of delegate Henry B. Stanton. The daughter of Daniel Cady, a judge of the New York Supreme Court, Elizabeth was pretty, robust, self-confident, and well educated. The only shadow on her privileged youth had been her realization that nothing she could ever do or accomplish would make up to her adored father for the death of his only son at age eighteen. The Cady household was politically conservative, but Elizabeth was a frequent visitor at the home of her cousin, Gerrit Smith, a wealthy philanthropist involved in

most of the reform causes of the day. He was a strong abolitionist and one of the founders of the antislavery Liberty
party. At Smith's house Elizabeth heard the vital issues of the
day discussed and met interesting radicals, among them
Henry Stanton, whom she soon married over the disapproval
of her family. Attendance at the World's Anti-Slavery Convention was part of their honeymoon trip.

At the convention Elizabeth struck up what became a lifelong friendship with Lucretia Mott, the fifty-five-year-old
Quaker minister with liberal opinions in theology and radical
ideas on the equality of women. Already filled with protofem-
inist ideas, Elizabeth was enthralled by the older woman. She
had found someone she could talk to about the books she had
been reading, like Mary Wollstonecraft's, and about her
doubts concerning the stern Presbyterian creed she had been
brought up in. She had never heard a woman speak in public
until she went to hear Mott preach at a Unitarian church in
London. "Mrs. Mott was to me an entire new revelation of
womanhood," she recalled later. On one of their sightseeing
walks they had determined that when they were back home
they would hold a convention and form a society to advocate
the rights of women. It was eight years before they could fulfill that promise.

As that eight-year gap indicates, while the relationship between the antislavery movement and the development of a
women's rights movement was strong, it was not a simple
matter of one leading directly into the other. Most of the
many women who became involved in the antislavery movement did not make the step into women's rights. All the early
leaders of the women's rights movement, and probably most
of their followers, were certainly antislavery in conviction
and had some involvement with that movement. But of the
major women leaders of the abolitionist movement, only Lu-

cretia Mott became an equally prominent leader of women's rights.

Even so, abolitionism was of vital importance to the emergence and growth of the women's movement. By appealing to women on religious and benevolent grounds to work for the most oppressed of all Americans, the slave, it drew in women who could never have responded to the secular rationalism of Fanny Wright. Yet by emphasizing liberty and equality it also led many of its adherents beyond the work of benevolence to self-examination and self-liberation. The movement provided an education in the processes of agitation and propaganda, and in analyzing the structure of institutions. It provided a milieu of religious fervor, but it was not afraid to attack the churches as institutions or dispute the standard clerical interpretations of the Bible. At the same time the opposition *within* the movement to women's assumption of a wider sphere of activity and authority brought home to many women the real weakness of their position.

Among numerous reform causes being agitated during the 1840s in the Northern states, marriage became a subject of intense public discussion. Many avant-garde middle-class people were impressed by the works of the French socialist Charles Fourier, whose ideas for a total reorganization of society along harmonious communitarian lines also involved breaking the chain of economic dependence that bound wives to husbands. Women would instead be afforded a range of occupations outside of conventional domestic drudgery and child-rearing. When the *New York Tribune* aired Fourier's philosophy, packaged for American consumption, many people were attracted to the idea of "associated" communitarian living. By 1845 there were at least twenty-six communities loosely based on Fourier's ideas in the Northeast, Midwest, Pennsylvania, and

Ohio. Most of them lasted only a year or two, but all attempted to some extent to free women from narrow domesticity and dependence on individual men. The discussion they ignited helped draw attention to women's situation in the modern social economy and stimulated debate on how this might be improved.

The consciousness of middle-class women was also raised by a movement for legal reform of the property rights of married women. Apart from enlistment in the army or navy, marriage was the only contractual relationship in nineteenth-century America in which one of the parties was expected to surrender many of the civil rights she had hitherto enjoyed. While single, women had the same right of inheritance, ownership of property, and contract as men, but once married their legal rights were strictly curtailed. The common-law term for a wife was *feme covert*, literally a covered or protected woman. The much-quoted English legal authority Sir William Blackstone had declared that "by marriage, the husband and wife are one person in law: that is, the very being or legal existence of the woman is suspended during the marriage, or at least is incorporated . . . into that of the husband."

In practical terms this meant that any personal property, money, or goods a woman brought to her marriage, or inherited after it, belonged entirely to her husband, to do with as he wished and to bequeath as he wished. Any real estate she already owned or inherited passed entirely under his control. On the husband's death, his widow was entitled to only one-third of her husband's real estate during her lifetime, and one-third of his personal property—though the latter could be bestowed differently by his will. It was possible for farsighted fathers to set up trusts for their daughters' property by prenuptial agreement, but not all states allowed such arrangements, and in any case they seem to have been used only by the very wealthiest families.

Even the money that a married woman might earn through wage work was considered to belong to her husband. He could collect her wages and use them even if the pair were living apart. This was because once married, all a woman's services were legally assumed to belong to her husband. A married woman could not make a valid will and could not enter into a contract. The husband was the sole legal guardian of the children of the marriage, and in his will he might appoint another guardian for them instead of the mother. In case of divorce or separation, the father, not the mother, was the preferred legal custodian of the children, though in practice some judges gave custody to the mother. The husband was legally responsible for his wife's behavior and was entitled to restrict her movements and "moderately" correct her. The other side of all this was that the husband was legally bound to support his wife, including in cases of legal separation and divorce, and to pay any debts she had acquired before marriage.

None of this was of primary concern to most women as long as their marriage was reasonably happy and the husband reasonably prosperous. But if he suffered economic reverses, if he spent her money as well as his own on drink or gambling, or if he deserted her, she might find herself and her children reduced to poverty, even if she had begun married life as an heiress. A widow might discover that her husband had died deeply in debt and that all the family property, including her home, could be seized by his creditors. A deserted wife who became self-supporting might suddenly find that her husband had returned to take any earnings or small property she had accumulated.

By the late 1820s a number of lawyers were beginning to demand reform of this draconian state of affairs. The question of married women's legal rights seemed to be a question that initially excited more interest among men than among women. An exception was a newcomer to America, Ernestine Rose, a young Jewish woman from Poland. Rose came to America in 1836, already a radical and already a feminist. At sixteen she had defied her rabbi father who had attempted to marry her to a much older man. She had left home the next year and gone to England, where she had become involved with the socialist movement around Robert Owen, and had married. She had also become economically independent by inventing a kind of scented air freshener.

When Rose and her husband moved to America, they quickly became part of radical free-thought circles in New York. When radical lawyer Thomas Herttell introduced a married women's property bill into the New York legislature, Rose tried to drum up support by circulating a petition among women in the state. As she later admitted ruefully, she obtained exactly five signatures. "Some of the ladies said the gentlemen would laugh at them; others that they had rights enough; and the men said the women had too many rights already." The bill failed, and failed again when Herttell reintroduced it in 1840.

More progress was made elsewhere. Mississippi and Maryland had already passed fairly limited married women's property acts that exempted property brought to the marriage by the wife from being taken by creditors to pay the debts of the husband. In the 1840s Maine, Massachusetts, Iowa, Michigan, Ohio, Indiana, Vermont, and Rhode Island all passed similar legislation. In New York the question was not allowed to die after 1840; bills were introduced almost yearly between 1843 and 1848. Ernestine Rose, with another future leader of the women's rights movement, Paulina Wright (Davis), continued to collect petitions and managed to persuade more women as well as men to sign. Finally in April 1848 a bill was passed as part of a comprehensive legal overhaul, securing to a married woman separate ownership and control of any property she brought into a marriage and any she inherited after it. Not until 1860 did New York extend this protection to any money she might *earn* while married. While most women had not been willing to agitate for legal change, once it was accomplished they began to take their new rights for granted. As Ernestine Rose recalled rather bitterly, "No sooner did it become legal than all the women said, 'Oh! that is right! We ought always to have had that.'"

These various state measures of the 1840s and 1850s, and others that followed during and after the Civil War, constituted the major *legal* change for women in the nineteenth century. These acts were also a prime example of how major reforms can be achieved by the convergence of quite differing strands of concern. The earliest acts, in Mississippi and Maryland, were a pragmatic response to economic distress, intended to prevent families from being wiped out by debt. Later acts in Northern states also reflected the desire of legal reformers to eliminate the more feudal aspects of the English common law, the interest of wealthy fathers in protecting their heiress daughters, and a humanitarian concern to protect dependent women and children. Some of the measures' major advocates, like Herttell, had a clearly feminist intent, and in some states lobbying by women was important in winning legislative support for reform. In Vermont, for example, the main impetus came from the editor of the *Windham County Democrat*, Clarina Howard Nichols, whose editorials spurred action in the legislature in 1847. In Pennsylvania the same year, passage of an act owed something to the sharp editorials of the feminist newspaper owner Jane Gray Swisshelm, supported by active petitioning organized by Lucretia Mott and other antislavery Quaker women. In Illinois in 1860, women who later became feminist leaders in that state served their apprenticeship by successfully lobbying for a married women's property act. In New York state too, the lobbying and petitioning from feminist advocates was an important part of the general swelling of support for reform.

But many strongly antifeminist women also favored property reform. Sarah Hale, for example, supported such legislation on grounds of justice and because she considered it was a chivalrous reform initiated by men to confer benefits on women. Once these basic measures of justice were secured, "we trust," she wrote in *Godey's*, "our sex will be intent only on performing their own duties." Horace Greeley, the influential editor of the *New York Tribune*, felt that concessions on practical "wrongs," like the property laws, was a way of deflecting women from more global equality claims, particularly in politics. Others felt that where laws clearly were unjust to women, "a temperate discussion of the principles of the law" would gradually bring reform, without any need for "clamors for rights, nor Amazonian intrepidity in claiming or defending them." Nonetheless the publicity surrounding these legal changes prompted a discourse about women that was formulated in terms of their property *rights*.

For most mainstream reformers, the question of women's involvement in politics seems to have been the dividing line between moderate reform and radicalism. Most (though not all) men who supported married women's property rights quickly dissociated themselves from any claims to political rights for women. The vast majority of women agreed. Politics and government were men's business, and besides, democratic politics were so rowdy, so full of partisan conflict that they were no place for delicate and retiring ladies. A number of developments in antebellum America made politics the prime distinguishing line of separation between the roles of men and of women. Between 1820 and 1850 state after state abolished property qualifications and made all white men eligible to vote—while sometimes disfranchising black males who had previously voted. A brief period of female voting in New Jersey after the Revolution had ended in 1807; now all women were excluded from the franchise. Thus, in terms of voting, the lines of sex and race were more tightly and explicitly drawn. In these same years party organization became increasingly sophisticated at turning out voters at election time and creating constant political excitement. Politics was a highly visible, exciting world—and a world of men.

Even so, by the 1840s women were becoming more visible on the political scene. In the presidential campaign of 1840 the Whig party made a special appeal to women for their moral support. Special areas were set aside for women to attend Whig rallies, and in the carefully orchestrated political processions attractive young women appeared on the floats. This was a kind of recognition of women as part of the polity. Still, their relation to the real game of politics remained analogous to the role of cheerleaders at a football game. Some women were prepared to demand a more serious role. When New York state revised its constitution in 1846, it received at least three petitions from women for women's suffrage.

A bold plea for political power for women had already been made three years earlier in a much-publicized speech in New York City by the novelist and journalist John Neal. Neal was by nature drawn to causes that would set the respectable public by its ears. He had given his first speech on women's rights as the 4th of July orator in Portland, Maine, in 1833. In it, he claimed later, "I exhausted the subject, and laid a foundation for about all the arguments I have heard since in favor of woman's rights." Ten years later he spoke to a packed house in

New York City, with the same message: the essential slavery of women.

Whether or not white women were slaves, he conceded, depended on how one defined slavery. But "that they are not *free—free*, in the sense that Men are *free* . . . is undeniably true." Yet surely it was *not* true that there could be "two kinds of Liberty—one for Man, and another for Woman." By freedom, the Founding Fathers had meant the power of self-government. Men had deprived women of this power through the "original accident of superior strength" and had used their mastery to devastating psychological as well as physical effect: "After monopolizing all power, [men] have extinguished her ambition, dwarfed her faculties, and brought her up to believe . . . that she was created only for the pleasure of man." The *Tribune* reported the speech on its front page, commenting that "this whole theory of 'The Rights of Women' is too absurd to argue against." The correspondent of the *National Intelligencer* wrote that Neal's "extravagant opinions" had been hissed by the women in the audience—"very fair data for the conclusion that ladies in this country have quite as much liberty as they desire."

Undaunted, Neal published his lecture in the popular magazine he edited, *Brother Jonathan*. This elicited a long reply from the writer and reformer Eliza Farnham, and led to a debate in the columns of the magazine that lasted over several issues. Farnham's main point was that yes, indeed, there *was* a different liberty for men and for women. "To be equally free is not to be free to do and enjoy the *same things*, but to be equally free" to follow one's essential nature. The physical and mental nature of women, and the nature of their domestic duties, unfitted them to perform in the business, professional, or political world. Women's "Declaration of Rights" was to be able to say, "I am a wife and mother. To be these is my freedom—to be other would be slavery." "To be free," she concluded, woman "must be allowed to preserve her distinctive sphere of action—in short, to be *woman*, not *man*."

Neal shot back that the essential issue was one of power. Like later feminists, he linked the economic hardships of women to their lack of political rights. "The social position of our women, we say, *depends upon their political position, and upon nothing else.* Just so long as they have no vote—no power—and are ineligible to office . . . they will be paid sixpence to a shilling a day for the same labor which a man would receive two or three dollars for."

The positions taken by Neal and Farnham in this early magazine dispute of 1843 prefigured the outlines of the debate over women's rights for the rest of the century. Neal's insistence on the importance of *political* power for real liberty and equality was a new note; it had not been so central for either Fanny Wright or the Grimkés.

Nor was it so central to the most important woman intellectual of the period, Margaret Fuller, who in 1845 published her reflections on the Woman Question in *Woman in the Nineteenth Century*. The daughter of a New England congressman, Fuller had received from her father one of those intense nineteenth-century hothouse educations in classic and modern languages and literature that were commonplace for young men but rare for girls. Her father, she recalled in a fictionalized account of her upbringing, "cherished no sentimental reverence for Woman, but a firm belief in the equality of the sexes. From the time she could speak and go alone, he addressed her not as a plaything, but as a living mind." This education endowed the grown-up Margaret with a firm conviction of her own high intellectual capabilities—but, as a woman, with no obvious field in which they could be used and further developed.

By her early twenties she was a member of the intellectual transcendentalist circle around Ralph Waldo Emerson. She could hold her own in that circle, but in looking at the intelligent and educated women she knew, it seemed to her that most of them were stultified by the lack of any real outlet for their abilities. They were victims of the general assumption that women's intellectual abilities should "be kept in the shade and never exhibited or displayed." In an attempt to remedy this (as well as support herself and her mother and siblings after the death of her father), in 1839 she began a series of public fee-paying Conversations for adult women in Boston, a cross between an adult education class and a seminar. Those who attended were expected to participate, to write short pieces as a basis for group discussion, and to develop the art of conversation, not as feminine chitchat or an exchange of personal confidences but as sustained and intelligent discussion of such intellectual themes as "Education," "Ethics," "Woman," and "Persons who never awake to life in this world." Too many of these latter were women. Fuller aimed to "raise the consciousness" of women and spur them to take themselves seriously. Above all she wished to prod women into thinking critically, and self-critically, rather than passively absorbing conventional wisdom.

Fuller carried on her program of Conversations for five years, involving some two hundred women. The Conversations attracted the intellectual elite of Boston women, those who were already entertaining a critical stance toward many aspects of their society. Even these women had been timid about speaking at first, perhaps overawed by Fuller's formidable reputation and her sometimes overbearing presence; perhaps, as one participant remarked during the Conversation on "Woman," because "women feared to trust their own thoughts . . . lest they should be wounded in heart." They quickly gained confidence, though, and the reminiscences of several of the participants indicate they found the experience inspiring and confidence-giving. "I found myself in a new world of thought," recalled one many years later. "Perhaps I could best express it by saying that I was no longer the limitation of myself, but I felt the whole wealth of the universe was open to me." Several women who attended the Conversations became involved with the women's rights movement: Caroline Healey Dall (at nineteen the youngest participant, whose notes supply much of what we know about the Conversations), and writers Julia Ward Howe, Ednah Dow (Littlehale) Cheney, and the antislavery writer Lydia Maria Child.

In *Woman in the Nineteenth Century* Fuller was in many ways continuing her Conversations in print, inviting her readers to think along with her, following the byways and diversions of her thought, searching "their own experience and intuitions" as they did so. In 1844 she had moved to New York and become a regular columnist for the *New York Tribune*, the first woman regularly employed by a major daily. Her experience of living and working in the great cosmopolitan center led to a new social awareness and the inclusion of a long discussion of prostitution in the book that some critics found "indelicate." Still, the starting point of her analysis was less woman as an oppressed human being than woman as a thwarted soul. "What woman needs," she wrote, was "as a nature to grow, as an intellect to discern, as a soul to live freely and unimpeded," to unfold her natural powers and capacities. This was an approach familiar in the transcendentalist circles that Fuller frequented. But to men like Emerson, the self-realizing individual was always male. Fuller applied the same precepts to women.

One of the most interesting aspects of Fuller's book was her concept of the dual nature of humanity in which male and female elements constantly pass and repass into each other, so that "there is no wholly masculine man, no purely feminine woman." The preponderance of gendered characteristics might differ as much from individual to individual as between men and women. This idea ran counter to the rigid categorization of sexual differences in most nineteenth-century discourse, and offered a way out of the straitjacket of dichotomous male/female natures without settling for an asexual identity.

Perhaps the central image in Fuller's book is an anecdote about a party of travelers who visit a lonely hut on a mountain. There they find an old woman who tells them she and her husband have lived there forty years. " 'Why,' they ask 'did you choose so barren a spot?' She 'did not know; *it was the man's notion.*' " "And during forty years," Fuller commented grimly, "she had been content to act, without knowing why, upon 'the man's notion.' I would not have it so." To Fuller this was just an extreme example of the general condition of women. Taught from an early age that they were not complete beings, they gave their minds as well as their material destinies over to their husbands, and from then on lived totally unexamined lives, without self-direction or self-awareness.

What was to be done? Men could help by removing "every arbitrary barrier" to women's self-realization, so that "every path" would be "laid open to Woman as freely as to Man." But liberation to Fuller was first and foremost internal and must be accomplished by women themselves. This process might involve a temporary withdrawal from men and marriage. Only when she had learned to be "self-centered" could a woman build a relationship with a man without being absorbed by it.

What would women do if all the "arbitrary barriers" were thrown down? Fuller conjured up an impatient, practical enquirer: "But if you ask me what offices they may fill; I reply—any . . . let them be sea-captains, if you will." This became one of Fuller's most quoted "sayings" and one that evoked great mirth. Her editor, Horace Greeley, delighted in quoting it to her whenever he thought she was betraying any "womanly weakness" (like insisting that she have a male escort through the night streets of New York to her home after working late at the *Tribune* office). But her point was simply that it was not for men to prescribe for women, or women to define for other women, what they could or could not do in life. Each individual must find and follow his or her own vocation.

Many people found Fuller's style in this book vague and high-flown, and her mix of mysticism and sharp analysis bewildering. Unsympathetic critics complained that it was hard to tell exactly *what* Fuller was demanding for women. Criticizing the work, John Neal wrote to her: "You go for thought—I for action. . . . I tell you that there is no hope for woman, till she has a hand in making the law—no chance for her till her *vote* is worth as much as a man's vote." Still, the first edition of *Woman in the Nineteenth Century* sold out within a week, and many women later dated the beginnings of their own "awakening" to reading her book.

A later leader of the women's rights movement, Paulina Wright Davis, said she always hoped that Fuller would become the leader of the cause. But in 1846 Fuller went to Europe, where she covered a revolution in Rome for the *Tribune*, married, and at age thirty-eight had a son. On returning to America in 1850 her ship foundered in sight of the shore, and Fuller, husband, and child were drowned. Even had she lived, her relation with the feminist movement would have been problematical. She was not a joiner, nor can one imagine her organizing conventions or lobbying state legislatures; she would have made an explosive mix with such other formidable egos as Elizabeth Cady Stanton and Susan B. Anthony.

Many years later these two women would hail Fuller as a "precursor," not for any specific program but as an inspiration for self-determination. Fuller spoke not as a planner but as a prophet. She believed the nineteenth century was a period of great opportunity and hope and that contemporary women were living at a decisive juncture in history. For that reason, what was needed was not "partial redress" of specific grievances but getting to "the root of the whole." "If principles could be established," she insisted, "particulars would adjust themselves aright." The founders of the soon-to-be-launched women's movement operated on the same premises. They would not be blind to the "particulars" of specific necessary reforms, but early feminism was fundamentally about a transformation of consciousness, of the ways in which men conceived of the capabilities and possibilities of women and, even more important, the ways in which women conceived of themselves.

3

Launching a Movement:
Seneca Falls and After

We hold these truths to be self-evident: that all men and
women are created equal.—Declaration of Sentiments,
Seneca Falls, 1848

A NEW PHASE of the Woman Question opened in July
1848 with the first convention ever called to agitate the rights
of women, in the small town of Seneca Falls, New York. The
prime mover was Elizabeth Cady Stanton, now thirty-three
years old and the mother of three young boys. On their return
to the United States the Stantons had settled in Boston, where
Henry opened a law office. Through her husband and her
new abolitionist contacts, Elizabeth met all the leading reformers of the day. Her role was still minor; she had begun to
speak to women's groups on Temperance and had conveyed
"homeopathic doses" of women's rights talk to them, as well
as circulating copies of Sarah Grimké's *Letters on the Equality
of Women*. In her personal life she was staking independent
positions. She and Henry had omitted the "obey" from their
marriage ceremony, and while she took her husband's last

name, quite soon after her marriage she began to insist on being called *Elizabeth Cady* Stanton, not, as was becoming increasingly the "correct" fashion, "Mrs. Henry Stanton." As she explained to a friend, "There is a great deal in a name. . . . The custom of calling women Mrs. John and Mrs. Tom, and colored men Sambo and Zip Coon, is founded on the principle that white men are lords of all"—something she refused to accept.

In 1847 Henry's political ambitions removed them to the small manufacturing town of Seneca Falls in upstate New York. Linked to major arteries of commerce, Seneca Falls was located in that region of New York state that had been labeled the "burned-over" district because it was so frequently swept by the fires of evangelical revivals and the reform movements that followed them. Two utopian communities had been established nearby; by the time the Stantons arrived, Seneca Falls had both antislavery and Temperance societies. Still, Seneca Falls was not Boston, and Cady Stanton missed the stimulating company and conversation she had known there. Her children were constantly sick, and she found it hard to get good household help. Henry was very often away for months at a time on legal business or pursuing his political plans. "I now fully understood," she wrote in her memoirs, "the practical difficulties most women had to contend with in the isolated household, and the impossibility of woman's best development if in contact, the chief part of her life, with servants and children." Personal discontent was now added to feminist convictions to form a potent charge.

The opportunity to light it came in July 1848, when she joined Lucretia Mott in a visit to Mott's sister and two other Quaker women in the nearby town of Waterloo. The visit turned into a consciousness-raising session, in which Cady Stanton poured out a torrent of her "long accumulating discontent" and so inspired the others that they determined then and there to take action. They decided to call a "convention" to discuss "the social, civil and religious rights of woman." They fixed on July 19 and 20 as the dates, secured the Wesleyan chapel in Seneca Falls as the place, and put a notice in the next day's local paper. They had left themselves very little time for arrangements, and none of them had any experience in organizing or conducting large-scale public meetings. But they had the example of the antislavery movement to draw upon. To women who were in the abolitionist reform culture, a public meeting of speeches and resolutions seemed the natural way to begin what they hoped would be a movement for sweeping social and political change.

The abolitionist societies also provided the model of a Declaration of Sentiments as a statement of principles to launch the movement. Cady Stanton had the happy inspiration of using the Declaration of Independence as a model, and the five women set about rewriting it to meet their own situation.* The opening paragraphs, with the famous universal declaration of natural rights, needed only minimal alterations. Finding analogues for George III and the list of his crimes was rather more difficult. "Man" was substituted for the king, as the oppressor of woman, and the women tried to compile the same number of grievances against man as the colonists had produced against the king.

The Declaration of Sentiments is not a parody, however. The women were appropriating one of the founding documents of their nation, and, like the abolitionists who also turned to the Declaration of Independence, forcing Americans to explore its implications. Before any specific proposals or reforms, feminism required women to stake their claim to

*It is reprinted in the Appendix to this book.

rank among those who are "created equal" and thus entitled to the consequent human rights. And while they were not contemplating setting up an independent nation of women, they *were* declaring their independence of men, in an exactly analogous fashion to the colonists declaring independence from George III. They were repudiating an authority over them that they had come to regard as both tyrannical and illegitimate. Like Jefferson's Declaration, too, the Sentiments and resolutions that emerged from Seneca Falls were not particularly new or original. They represented, if not yet the general enlightened sentiments of mankind, at least ideas which had been batted about in progressive and reforming circles for some twenty years.

Though the convention had been a spur-of-the-moment venture, the feeling that women's position needed rethinking was sufficiently widespread to bring a fair number of participants. The 19th was a broilingly hot July day, but the roads to Seneca Falls were soon crowded with wagons as people journeyed from outlying towns and even from Rochester, fifty miles away. About a hundred people attended the first day, and by the second some three hundred.

The meeting was presided over by James Mott, Lucretia's husband. None of the women organizers had the nerve to conduct a public meeting open to men and women, though both Lucretia Mott and Cady Stanton spoke. The Declaration of Sentiments was read, followed by a series of resolutions inviting the audience's assent. Most of these resolutions involved broad claims to equality and a wider sphere of action. One, in rather roundabout language, denounced the sexual double standard. Of the two that made explicit demands, one, that women have equal access to all trades and professions, including the ministry, was added at the last moment by Lucre-

tia Mott. The other, proposed by Cady Stanton, demanded the
vote.

When she had read that resolution to her husband before
the convention, he told her that such a proposal would turn
the proceedings into a farce. If she persisted in going through
with it he would leave town—which he did. All the other resolutions were passed by unanimous consent of the convention,
but many people balked at this one. Cady Stanton gave an im-
passioned speech (her maiden speech to a "mixed" audience)
in its defense. But she might not have carried the day had it
not been for the aid of Frederick Douglass. Douglass, the only
African American present, was an escaped slave who had already become a famous orator in antislavery circles. He and
Elizabeth Cady Stanton had met and become friends in
Boston. In 1847 he had moved to Rochester where he had set
up his own newspaper, the *North Star*. Douglass now added
his voice to Cady Stanton's, and the resolution for the vote was
narrowly passed.

After two days, participants were asked to sign the declaration as a token of agreement and commitment. One hundred
did so—sixty-eight women and thirty-two men—though in
the next few days, as an unexpected storm of press criticism
and ridicule broke about their ears, a number asked to have
their names removed. The signatures, however, enable historians to learn something not just about the leaders but about
the kinds of people who would make up the rank and file of
the coming women's movement. A study of the signers reveals
ages ranging from fourteen to sixty-eight, with a mean age of
just under thirty-nine. With the exception of Douglass, ethni-
cally the signers reflected the area from which they came,
which was still overwhelmingly white, native born, and
Protestant. They were broadly middle class, though there was

one male factory worker among them. Nineteen-year-old Charlotte Woodward, the only female signer who lived to cast a vote in 1920, was an artisan—a glove-maker. On average the signers were somewhat better off than most people in the area, but there was considerable variation. Only a third came from farms; the rest were from households involved in the manufacturing sector, professions, or trade.

The signers were linked in a number of already established networks. People tended to sign in family groups: husbands and wives, mothers and daughters, sisters. A high number were affiliated in some way with the new Free Soil antislavery party, and there was a large contingent of dissident Quakers, soon calling themselves Progressive Friends, who had split off from their more conservative brethren only the month before on issues of antislavery, religious authority, and freedom. Among those present but not signing was Temperance activist Amelia Bloomer, wife of a local lawyer. Not long after, Bloomer came round to the cause of women's rights, and a Temperance paper she had started, the *Lily*, became a vehicle for the cause and carried lively articles by Elizabeth Cady Stanton.

The convention received a good deal of free publicity from the press. Reform papers, like Douglass's, hailed the meeting. While there had been no delegations of factory workers at the convention, the *Factory Girl's Voice* published the Declaration of Sentiments in full, commenting that it was an "improved edition" of the Declaration of Independence and adding, "We rejoice in that Convention as a significant indication of the tendencies of this age."

But the main press reaction was astonishment mixed with ridicule. Headlines such as "Bolting Among the Ladies," "Women Out of Their Latitude," and "The Reign of Petticoats" were typical. The resolutions were "new, impracticable, absurd and ridiculous." "Every true hearted female will instantly feel that this is unwomanly," reproved the Albany *Mechanic's Advocate*. The *New York Herald* thought the whole thing very amusing, particularly the preamble to the declaration, which it nonetheless printed in full. The organizers, however, sensed that for a fledgling social movement any publicity was better than none. "Imagine the publicity given to our ideas by thus appearing in a widely circulated sheet like the *Herald*," crowed Cady Stanton to Mott. The ridicule of the press might deter some, but it spread the news that women had organized around the idea of women's rights, and that was enough to spur other groups of women to action.

The initiative quickly passed into new hands. So suddenly had the Seneca Falls meeting been got together that the organizers had no immediate plans to follow it up. But a mere two weeks later, in Rochester, another convention was called, organized by antislavery Quaker activist Amy Post, who had attended the Seneca Falls meeting. So swift was the process of radicalization that this time a woman took the chair, and from then on feminist women presided at their own meetings.

Seneca Falls marked a qualitative step forward in the evolution of the Woman Question. Earlier feminist statements had been the work of individuals, speaking and writing as individuals. Now a group of women were organizing as a collectivity and producing a group statement that invited public assent. The Seneca Falls convention and those that followed provided a focus for incohate discontent, and gave many women who were brooding over their inferior position and lack of opportunities not only the realization that they were not alone or odd, but that they could actually do something about it. No formal organized national society, with constitution and dues, emerged from Seneca Falls, but from 1848 onward there was something that could be called a women's movement in America.

How is a movement organized? how does it grow? how is the message spread? Several historians and sociologists have begun to examine the nineteenth-century women's rights movement through concepts derived from the sociology of social movements. The existence of grievances is not enough to explain the rise and persistence of a social protest movement, since grievances may exist for a long time without provoking an overt organized response. The key appears to lie rather in the emergence of some kind of organizational structure and a core leadership group that can articulate a compelling ideology and mobilize resources. These resources include money, access to instruments of publicity like the press, and the ability to take advantage of existing organizational and friendship networks as well as already circulating currents of thought and debate.

At the center of the new women's movement was a small core of recognized leaders who emerged in its early years. They had no formal organization and no hierarchy, and later personal and ideological rifts would develop. But until the Civil War they were linked by ties of personal friendship, some particularly strong, and varying degrees of common experience in other reform work, such as antislavery and Temperance. Above all, they were united by a common rage at the position of women and a common commitment to an ideology of emancipation. They coopted other women who attracted their attention and brought them into the loose leadership circle, along with a number of prominent male sympathizers. Similar leadership groups could be found at the state and local levels. These were the people who organized meetings, coordinated petition and lobbying campaigns, wrote for the press, and spoke constantly. A peripheral group of women writers were not involved in organization but were sympathetic and important as a means of spreading feminist ideas. These included the antislavery writer and journalist Lydia Maria Child, the novelist and columnist Ruth Parton (Fanny Fern), the journalist Grace Greenwood, and, for a while, the editor of the Pittsburgh *Saturday Vister*, Jane Swisshelm.

By the early 1850s the core leadership of the movement had crystallized. In addition to Elizabeth Cady Stanton and Lucretia Mott, it included Lucy Stone and her great friend from Oberlin days, Antoinette Brown, the first woman in America to be ordained as minister of an orthodox Congregational church; Caroline Dall (née Healey), who by the mid-1850s had revised her opinions on women's rights from her school days, and Harriot Hunt, one of the first women to practice medicine as a profession, both from Massachusetts; Paulina Wright Davis from Rhode Island; the writer Elizabeth Oakes Smith; and Elizabeth Jones and Frances Dana Gage from Ohio. Amelia Bloomer and the newspaper editor Clarina Howard Nichols of Vermont took their feminism west when they moved to Ohio and Kansas respectively during the decade. Ernestine Rose quickly attached herself to the new movement and became one of its most radical and effective speakers. The most important new recruit was undoubtedly Susan B. Anthony.

The daughter of a liberal Quaker father who had suffered considerable losses in the general panic of 1837, Anthony had taught school for ten years. It was not an experience she enjoyed. She bitterly resented the low wages of female teachers compared with those of men, and the male dominance of professional associations. The Anthony household near Rochester was involved in many of the reform causes of the 1830s and 1840s. Susan's father and one of her sisters had attended the second women's rights convention in Rochester in 1848 and had signed its resolutions.

Anthony herself was more involved with the antislavery movement and particularly with Temperance at this point, but reading a speech by Lucy Stone apparently converted her to the cause of women's rights. In 1851 she met Amelia Bloomer at a Temperance meeting, and Bloomer introduced her to Elizabeth Cady Stanton. This was the beginning of one of the great political partnerships in American history. By 1852, at age thirty-two, Anthony was not only attending her first women's rights convention but taking a major part in its proceedings.

Susan B. Anthony was a woman of ferocious dedication and commitment. She was never a great speaker or writer, but she was a superlative organizer. She threw herself into this new cause and soon found herself not only part of the core leadership but taking on much of the nuts and bolts of organizing. Unmarried, angular, rather grim looking, and somewhat abrasive, she was one of the few early feminists who resembled the stereotype developed by a hostile press. "She was a sort of scape-goat for all of us," admitted Antoinette Brown. With Stanton she developed a long, close friendship that survived disagreements over policy and the inevitable periods of coolness. It was a working partnership based on collaboration in advancing the cause of women as they saw it. In the beginning, Anthony was the one who could move about freely on lecture tours and petition-gathering expeditions, while Cady Stanton, confined at home with her children, often wrote many of Anthony's speeches.

A social movement operates on many different levels. It is given shape and direction by a visible, accepted leadership, but it rests on the activities of the many less visible workers. The reminiscences of Emily Collins, who never became a national figure but who was a lifelong soldier in the cause of women's rights, show how the spark could operate. Growing up in a remote area of New York state, she recalled, she had always rebelled against confining customs and "pined for that freedom of thought and action that was then denied to all womankind." When she read the lectures of Ernestine Rose and the writings of Margaret Fuller, "and found that other women entertained the same thoughts that had been seething in my own brain, and realized that I stood not alone, how my heart bounded with joy!" But it was the reports of the meeting at Seneca Falls that "gave this feeling of unrest form and voice." Inspired, she called together a few women of the neighborhood, and they formed a Woman's Equal Rights Union. They were a group of fifteen to twenty, most of them married like Collins, and probably around her age, about forty; a few were younger and single. They met every other week in someone's parlor to exchange ideas, and also introduced women's rights issues to the debating clubs that were then popular institutions in rural districts. They drafted a petition to the state legislature for women's suffrage and got sixty-two signatures, male and female, from their own and adjoining towns. The petition met only ridicule in Albany, but the women continued to send similar ones, though the formal group ceased to meet after about a year "on account of bad weather and the difficulty of coming together in the country districts."

In 1858 Collins moved to Rochester, where she found an existing feminist community. She joined it in a yearly petition to the legislature for women's suffrage, and wrote newspaper articles on women's rights. After the Civil War, when she and her husband moved to Louisiana, she became part of a small new women's rights movement there and in 1879 joined in a petition for suffrage to the state constitutional convention. Here is a record of dogged feminist activism pursued out of the limelight for more than thirty years by a woman who created or found small feminist groups when she moved from place to place. There must have been many Emily Collinses.

Until after the Civil War the women's movement was loosely coordinated by a central committee, with an annually appointed president who was responsible for organizing annual "national" conventions. There were some state societies, and numerous, often ephemeral, local groups. A few women's rights journals and tracts were published; individual activists toured on the lecture circuit; and various campaigns for legal reforms were directed at state legislatures. These modes of operation met the two broad goals of the movement. On the one hand feminists wanted a reform of laws and institutions that oppressed women, particularly married women; on the other they aimed to transform men's ideas about women, and women's ideas about themselves. The two goals were intertwined but demanded different tactics.

Reforming the law and winning the vote required persuading state legislators. The most available means were petition campaigns, plus lobbying. Numerous state campaigns of this kind were conducted by core local activists, sometimes supplemented by speaking tours from national leaders. Occasionally, too, advocates would appear personally before a legislature to present petitions and speak for women's rights. In trying to gain concessions from government, the women's rights advocates were of course hampered by the lack of one of their major demands—the vote. They did not have the power to punish recalcitrant politicians at the polls, nor the clout to persuade the major political parties to adopt any of their demands as party planks. Nor, like some antislavery men by the 1840s, could they organize a separate political party.

On a different level, however, all the leaders assumed that changing institutions partly depended on—even followed from—a necessary fundamental change in public opinion. Ultimately the emancipation of women depended upon transforming both men's and women's ideas about women's nature, capabilities, and roles. Toward this end the women instinctively adopted the techniques they were familiar with from the antislavery movement—extensive use of the press, lecture platform, and public meetings.

This was a period when the public meeting was a major fixture of American civilization. The philosopher Jurgen Habermas has described the development in the late eighteenth century of a particular kind of "public sphere"—an arena consisting of the press, journals, clubs, and public assemblies, in which men outside of government or priestly office could nonetheless freely debate issues of public importance and make their opinions known. Such a public sphere depended on two things: first, that state institutions should allow freedom of speech and assembly, and, second, that there should be a general political culture in which a large number of men should feel themselves entitled and empowered to discuss issues in this way. The core personnel of the public sphere were the new and growing middle class. In democratic America, where the middle class was proportionately more numerous than in Europe, this public sphere was very large. It was, however, male.

When women's rights advocates claimed access to the press, when they gave well-publicized lectures, and when they staged women's rights conventions they were dramatically asserting women's right also to act in this public sphere, and to present for public scrutiny and debate matters of fundamental social and political importance—indeed, to maintain that the *position of women* was a matter of fundamental public importance and determination, not an immutable ordinance of nature.

After the conventions at Seneca Falls and Rochester there was a pause of more than a year, but in 1850 and 1851 conventions were called in Ohio, at Salem and Akron. The Salem convention produced a "memorial" to the Ohio constitutional convention, bearing eight thousand signatures and asking that the new constitution enshrine "equal rights ... without distinction of sex or color." Also in 1850 a call went out for a "national" convention to be held in Worcester, Massachusetts. This was the work of thirty-seven-year-old Paulina Wright Davis, the wife of a wealthy manufacturer. She already had an extensive reform career; she had been recruited by Abby Kelley to lecture on the antislavery circuit, and with Ernestine Rose she had distributed petitions for married women's property rights. After the death of her first husband, she had struck out on her own in the late 1840s, lecturing widely to women's groups on physiology and women's health. An attractive woman, with a very feminine manner which disarmed criticism, Davis had extensive contacts among "advanced" and reform circles. She sent notices of the convention to all of them, asking their presence or endorsement.

In terms of creating a movement, the Worcester meeting may have been more important than Seneca Falls. It drew people from nine different states and featured a number of speakers who had already made a name for themselves in the world of reform. One of the stars was Lucy Stone, who was now supporting herself as a public lecturer on antislavery and women's rights. She had given her first women's rights lecture in her brother's church in 1847, even before Seneca Falls. Unlike Davis, she was not particularly impressive in appearance, but she had a beautiful speaking voice and the power to tame hostile audiences.

The Worcester meeting was more widely reported in the press than the earlier conventions and was even noted by

English newspapers. It inspired Harriet Taylor Mill, the wife of the political philosopher John Stuart Mill, to write a highly influential essay in the *Westminster Review* on "The Enfranchisement of Women." It was widely circulated in America where it became a major movement document. News of the movement also drew a spark in France, where the Revolution of 1848 had inspired the hopes of a small group of socialist feminists. These hopes were soon dashed, and by 1851 its leaders were in prison. From there two of them wrote a letter to the next convention pledging solidarity from "your socialist sisters of France" and urging the American women to take up the cause of labor. Other prominent European women also sent statements of support. All this gave the American women the buoyant feeling that, however small a minority they might be, they were part of an international movement of progressive historical forces.

The 1850 convention launched the idea that there should be a yearly "national" convention, and one was in fact held every year up to the Civil War, with the exception of 1857, in locations including Worcester again in 1851; Syracuse, New York, in 1852; Cleveland in 1853; Philadelphia in 1854; Cincinnati in 1855; and New York in 1856, 1858, 1859, and 1860. The number of people attending grew each year: two thousand came in 1852, and the New York meetings attracted even larger audiences. Additional state and local conventions continued to be held from time to time, depending on the availability and energy of local leaders or a particular state political situation. Conventions were often timed to coincide with state constitutional conventions.

The conventions brought people together from different locales, helped overcome isolation, and enabled new networks to be forged. As rituals of commitment they boosted morale, confirmed the faithful, and brought in new recruits. Activist

Frances Dana Gage of Ohio, a newspaper columnist and mother of eight, attended the women's rights conventions in Ohio and Philadelphia in 1852. In a letter to the *Lily* she defended women like herself who were criticized for leaving home for a week to gad off to a convention. "We are isolated," she wrote, "and so few in number, struggling against such fearful odds, that we grow weary, faint of heart, and relax our energy. We long to meet sympathizers—to see others who think as we think, feel as we feel," and regain courage from that contact.

One important feature of the movement was the presence of men. While man might be the oppressor, individual men could be friends and allies. A number of sympathetic lawyers and legislators could be counted on to draft legislation and present petitions. Men prominent in reform circles also regularly attended women's rights conventions and wrote and spoke on their behalf. The most important were the black leaders Frederick Douglass and Robert Purvis; liberal clergymen Theodore Parker, Thomas Wentworth Higginson, William Henry Channing, and Samuel May; the abolitionist William Lloyd Garrison; and the upper-class radical Wendell Phillips. Businessman and reformer Henry Blackwell, brother of the pioneer woman doctor Elizabeth Blackwell, gave his first speech for women's rights at the Cleveland convention of 1853 and became increasingly active in the movement after his marriage two years later to Lucy Stone. John Neal maintained an interest in the movement, and by the late 1850s there were two prestigious new recruits—Henry Ward Beecher, brother of Catharine and probably the most famous evangelical preacher in America, and the journalist George William Curtis. These men, though controversial, were figures of considerable prestige in those progressive circles in which the women's movement operated. Thus these conventions, quite

apart from what was said at them, in their structure exemplified a major aspect of the women's movement philosophy:
breaking down and dissolving the spheres. The conventions
were a demonstration that men and women could collaborate
as equals publicly and asexually outside the family.

Conventions featured addresses from a fairly limited roster
of speakers and offered considerable opportunity for audience
participation and debate. Resolutions were offered for assent,
mainly variations on those first presented at Seneca Falls. The
conventions demanded equal educational opportunities for
women; equal access to well-paid and prestigious work, including all the trades and professions; a removal of the injus-
tices of marriage, making husbands and wives equal in law
with respect to property and guardianship of children; and finally the vote—as a matter of justice, since single women or
widows with property were taxed without representation, but
also, increasingly, as the key that would enable women to win
many of the other things they wanted. The emphasis among
these various demands varied somewhat from convention to
convention, but the program was essentially the same.

The movement relied on the written as well as the spoken
word. Major speeches were sometimes published separately, as
were the proceedings of most of the national and several of the
state conventions. There was no major feminist philosopher to
produce an authoritative treatise, but Elizabeth Oakes Smith's
Woman and Her Needs (1851) and Caroline Dall's published
lectures, *The College, the Market, and the Court* (1867) provided
extended treatments of some aspects of emerging feminist
thought.

Several fairly short-lived periodicals were also founded as
organs for the movement. The *Lily* lasted until 1855, with six
thousand subscribers. In 1853 Paulina Wright Davis founded
the *Una*, which never had more than five hundred subscribers

and folded within two years. A Philadelphia journal, the *Woman's Advocate*, owned by a joint-stock company of women, ran for two years from 1855 to 1857, and the *Sybil*, which was particularly interested in dress and health reform, was published in New York state from 1856 to 1864. The journals reached women who could not attend conventions or public meetings and reassured them, as one wrote to the *Sybil*, "that I am not alone in the world." They published articles, news of progress for women—or particularly dramatic examples of their wrongs, and letters from readers. Paulina Davis thought the letters were especially important. "One letter in print from some worn and weary spirit does more to develop and help woman out of her weakness than ever so many private complaints," she told her coeditor Caroline Dall. Much of the nation's antislavery press could also be counted on for favorable and substantial coverage of the conventions, sometimes reprinting entire speeches.

To reach beyond the converted, the movement relied on exposure in major newspapers and always made sure that reporters were invited to the conventions. An extensive study of the reporting of women's rights activities during this period concludes that newspapers devoted considerable space to the topic and that this publicity was crucial for the movement. The three major New York dailies, the *New York Tribune*, the *New York Times*, and the *New York Herald,* were especially important, since their reports were often picked up by newspapers elsewhere. Some papers, like Horace Greeley's *New York Tribune*, were quite supportive; many, particularly James Gordon Bennett's *New York Herald*, were adamantly, even viciously, opposed. "That motley gathering of fanatical mongrels, of old grannies, male and female, of fugitive slaves and fugitive lunatics ..." began a *Herald* report on the Worcester convention. The *Herald* thought the women's movement was aiming at nothing less than revolution, involving socialism, interracial sex, and atheism.

Most papers devoted a good deal of attention to the personal appearance of the women's rights speakers. Sympathetic reporters emphasized that the women were "womanly," sweet-voiced, and not unattractive. Hostile reporters described them as thin (not a compliment in the nineteenth century), bony, hatchet-faced, "screeching," "gabbling," and "clamoring." To the sympathetic, the women were making a startling but—it had to be admitted—rational claim to justice. To the hostile, they were involved in the absurd attempt to overturn the settled order of nature. A major aspect of hostile press reports was the accusation that women who talked about women's rights were somehow "unsexed." They were "amazons," "hybrids," or—in the curious epithet of the day—"strong-minded" (with the unavoidable implication that the true feminine woman must be "weak-minded"!). They must certainly be disappointed old maids, and sometimes the reporter hoped they might be cured of their feminism by a good husband and a bouncing baby.

Male supporters of the movement were special targets of press abuse. While the women were denounced as masculine, male feminists were branded as effeminate, "Aunt Nancy men." Even the mildest endorsement of a women's rights position by a man might prompt jeers of effeminacy. This reaction to the male feminists suggests the reason for the often hysterical opposition to the women's rights movement. Women who were demanding equal rights with men, and particularly the right to take part in the public sphere, were proposing to invade male turf. This could only mean ultimately an inversion of nature and a reversal of roles. If women did the things that men did, would not this mean that they would *become* like men, and then—the ultimate hor-

ror!—would not men become like women? Public antifeminist discourse, from newspaper editorials to cartoons to comic
songs, was filled with dire images of women wearing
breeches, smoking cigars, and striding off to the saloon or the
political rally while their miserable, downtrodden husbands
stayed home to do the laundry and look after the baby. Any
male who supported feminist goals must be a traitor to his sex,
not a real man.

Many hostile press responses also betrayed discomfort with
the idea of female *bodies* as part of the public sphere. *New York
Herald* editorials were particularly egregious in this respect.
"How funny it would sound," wrote Bennett, in what was
clearly intended to be the ultimate putdown, if Lucy Stone, as
a lawyer in the midst of arguing a case, was suddenly taken by
the pangs of childbirth and "gave birth to a fine bouncing boy
in court!" Such remarks, and the many nervous jokes about
role reversal, now seem bizarre. Still, extremists sometimes
perceive a kernel of truth denied to more sober and moderate
conservatives. In the twentieth century the involvement of
women in politics has produced not a baby on the Senate floor
but certainly a change in the kinds of subjects that politics is
supposed to be about. Questions involving children and issues
of reproduction have become part of the political and legal
world in a way that would have been utterly foreign to the
politicians of the mid-nineteenth century. Similarly, feminists
in the late twentieth century have realized that an equal role
for women in the public world of work does require more involvement by men in child care and domestic life.

The general social preoccupation with women's appearance
had repercussions in the movement. Clothes, like names, have
considerable symbolic importance. From the 1850s on, while
men's clothes were becoming more austere, fashionable

woman's dress was becoming more elaborate. Nineteenth-century feminists constantly criticized women for their vanity and preoccupation with dress. These concerns, they argued, prevented women from concentrating their minds on more important matters, led to extravagance, and only fed the male image of woman as a "butterfly" who could scarcely be entrusted with the serious business of the world. An unspoken consensus emerged from the earliest women's rights meetings that women at them would dress simply, as a sign they were serious people. The large contingents of Quaker women at these affairs helped set the tone.

There was no "policy" on the matter, but its emotional importance was made startlingly clear at the Syracuse convention of 1852. Paulina Davis had invited the well-known Boston author Elizabeth Oakes Smith, who had already written several articles on women's rights, with the intention of having her elected president of the central committee for the next year. Unfortunately the new recruit turned up at the evening meeting of the convention straight from a party, wearing an elaborate, low-cut evening dress. This caused a good deal of muttering. Susan Anthony, who was attending her first women's rights convention, was outraged. She insisted that a woman who dressed like that could not represent "the earnest, solid hardworking women of this country." Smith's nomination was voted down.

This was a tempest within the movement, but the question of dress created a storm of publicity with the emergence in 1851 of the famous "bloomer" costume. This style was given the name of bloomer by the press because it was first publicized in Amelia Bloomer's *Lily*, though it was actually invented by Gerrit Smith's daughter Elizabeth Miller. It consisted of a shortish dress, to the knees or mid-calf, worn over either full "Turkish" trousers gathered at the ankle, or straight pants. The waist was loose and natural, and the dress was worn without corsets.

Women's dress styles of the mid-nineteenth century came under attack from several quarters. Men constantly complained about the sheer amount of *room*—in the streets, on trains, or in theaters—taken up by the huge skirts women wore by the 1850s; many women also found these long skirts increasingly irksome. They were heavy, impeded movement, and were constantly trailing in the dust and dirt of unpaved streets. Doctors, women like Catharine Beecher, and others concerned with women's health were also mounting campaigns against tight-laced corsets, complete with horror stories about displaced internal organs that made healthy motherhood impossible. Thus "dress reform" was one of the many issues that were in the air and not specifically feminist. The bloomer might seem an ideal solution. Many women—not only women's rights activists—were attracted by the freedom of movement the new costume offered.

But not for long. The costume produced a storm of ridicule. Women wearing bloomers were greeted with catcalls and rude remarks in the street. Comic songs about bloomers appeared in the music halls. Caricaturists had a field day—and from then on feminists were usually portrayed wearing the bloomer costume. Though the dress was extremely modest, it was denounced from the pulpit not so much for the short skirt but for the trousers worn underneath it. Women, it was said, were unsexing themselves and appropriating male dress—just one more indication that the women's movement really aimed to usurp male roles. Elizabeth Cady Stanton's two oldest sons at boarding school pleaded with her not to visit them wearing bloomers! She replied that she understood: "You want me to be like other people." But, she added, "you must learn not to care for what foolish people say."

Easier said than done. Cady Stanton was one of the first to give up what she always affectionately referred to as "the shorts." Lucy Stone and Anthony reluctantly followed suit. By 1854–1855 all the major feminist leaders had gone back to conventional dress. The bloomer soon all but disappeared, though it was still sometimes worn by farm women, pioneers on the overland trail, and the occasional diehard feminist.

While the press was finding good copy, feminist leaders were experiencing all the practical problems that bedevil organizers. One concern that emerged early on in the conventions was the question of women's voices. Since artificial amplification was not yet available, speakers at a public meeting had to be able to project to the back of the hall. Men with a high school or college education were trained in public speaking, women were not. What's more, the current notions of femininity required women to speak softly. A lifetime's training in self-effacement, together with understandable nervousness at facing the public for the first time, meant that many early women speakers could not be heard beyond the first rows. Catcalls and cries of "Louder!" and "Speak up!" from men and boys at the back did not help.

If it was difficult to get speakers to speak up, it was also hard to prevent them from running on. The trouble with the women speakers, a weary Anthony complained in 1859 to Caroline Dall, is that "each one always seems anxious to relieve herself of every straggling thought that ever found place in their heads. I do not wish to be rude or unkind, but I was so tired last year, with rambling *undigested talk* from the women." The conventions were deliberately designed as open forums to which anyone could come, opponents as well as friends, and offer testimony or arguments. Inevitably some people would drone on while audiences grew restless, especially at long harangues from clerical opponents. But because they were ideologically committed to free speech, the presiding chairs were reluctant to cut anyone off. At one or two conventions there were serious disruptions from rowdies in the gallery who had been purposely recruited to shout down the speakers.

A particular stumbling block for these early conventions was religion. Orthodox clergy often attended in order to present biblical proof that God had created women to be silent and subject to men. Biblical authority was too important to too many women, including many convinced feminists, to be ignored. As a college student at Oberlin, Antoinette Brown had carefully studied the Scriptures in Greek to be able to show that the usual arguments on women's inferiority were misinterpretations. She became the major public spokeswoman to answer clerical attacks and also head off anything that seemed antireligious from within the movement. A heated debate occurred in Philadelphia in 1854 when Hannah Tracy Cutler of Illinois traded text for text with the antifeminist Reverend Henry Grew. But the main thrust of Cutler's speech reflected a tendency among movement leaders to back off from close engagement with biblical arguments in favor of the authority of inner conviction. "Too long have we learned God's will from the lips of man," she said, "and closed our eyes on the great book of nature and the safer teaching of our own souls." William Lloyd Garrison made the decisive intervention by demanding angrily, "Why go to the Bible" to settle this question? "What question was ever settled by the Bible? The human mind is greater than any book."

These attacks on clerical and biblical authority were taken up with glee by the press, which branded the women's movement with "infidelity" (the early-nineteenth-century term for atheism). They made a particular target of Ernestine Rose, who made no secret of being a Freethinker and anticlerical. Some movement women were also disturbed by Rose, either because they were genuinely distressed by her open lack of religion or because they feared she put the whole movement in a bad light and would frighten away church-committed women.

Keeping the issue constantly before the public; maintaining the momentum of conventions and other activities; and bringing in new recruits and keeping up morale required an extraordinary commitment of time and energy and of *self* from the core organizers. Not surprisingly, some suffered from burnout. Paulina Wright Davis in 1854 confessed that "the Conventions hang like a dead weight upon me from year to year." Anthony too, though determinedly upbeat, sometimes wondered whether all her effort was worth it. "Why are there *so few women workers?*" she complained to Stone in 1857. "Why do we not have *new women* coming on to the stage of public action?"

Women as public speakers were now less startling than the Grimkés had been, and the extensive lecture tours undertaken by some of the women could be highly profitable both in converts and in money. They could also be grueling. In the winter of 1855 Anthony stumped New York state, alone and with Ernestine Rose, speaking and gathering signatures for women's rights petitions. Many of the small towns they visited did not yet have rail connections, so much of their traveling was done by horse and buggy over dirt roads, by sleigh, or on foot. Anthony spoke twice a day, every other day, traveling in between and making all her own arrangements. Antoinette Brown on a tour in 1852 spoke eighteen times in nineteen days. On her return journey the stagecoach was full and left her behind; so, she reported laconically to Lucy Stone, she started to walk, hitched a ride for about two miles, then walked the remaining "7 1/2 through the snow in the midst of a big snow storm." She arose the next morning feeling fine except for a sore toe, but the physical hardship took its toll on others, as did the mental effort of having to be continually prepared for meetings.

A major problem was the pull of domestic responsibilities. Leading figures such as Cady Stanton, Lucy Stone, and Antoinette Brown Blackwell were in their prime childbearing years. Lucy Stone had assumed she would never marry, but in 1855 at age thirty-seven she did so, to the antislavery worker Henry Blackwell, and had a daughter the following year. Blackwell followed the example of Robert Dale Owen and Theodore Weld, repudiating the legal power over his wife given him by the law. Stone went a step further and retained her own name: she was to be known as Mrs. Lucy Stone. This was an unprecedented step and prompted extensive comment. It was Stone's symbolic assertion that her individuality would not be swallowed up and submerged by marriage.

Like the Grimké-Welds before them, the Stone-Blackwells did not intend marriage to interfere with the wife's career as a speaker and reformer. But in fact, though her withdrawal was considerably less final than Angelina Grimké's, after the birth of her child Stone did remove herself for some five years from active involvement in public work. "I wish I felt the old impulse & power to lecture," she wrote wistfully to Antoinette in 1859, after attending an inspiring talk on Joan of Arc. But when she thought of all the evils that might befall her child in her absence, "I shrank like a snail into its shell, & saw that for these years I can be only a mother." Antoinette Brown married Henry's brother Samuel in 1856 and quickly produced five daughters. She too found it difficult to continue the ambitious program of preaching and lecturing on women's rights that she had mapped out for herself.

Elizabeth Cady Stanton had four more children between 1845 and 1859, making seven in all. She continued to publish articles and letters and made major presentations to the New York legislature in 1854 and 1860, but she could not travel much and was unable to attend most of the prewar conventions, sending letters in lieu of speeches. Usually she sailed through her pregnancies without much trouble, but when pregnant with her last child in 1858, she had to cancel an important speaking engagement in Boston because she felt so drained. She was so embarrassed that she devised an excuse that her speech had been lost in stolen luggage. "As the Maternal difficulty has always been one of the arguments against woman entering public life," she confessed to Elizabeth Miller, "I did not like the idea that I, who had a hundred times declared the difficulty to be absurd, should illustrate in my own person the contrary thesis. It was all too humiliating." She was a devoted mother, but she felt keenly her lack of freedom, especially compared with her husband, who was still frequently absent on political business. "I pace up and down these two chambers of mine like a caged lioness," she wrote in 1856. No wonder she saw menopause as freedom: "We shall not be in our prime until 50," she told Anthony, "and then we will have a good twenty years left."

The rise of Susan B. Anthony to a dominant position within the feminist movement was due in part to the fact that alone among the major leaders she remained unmarried. She had nothing to interfere with her dedication or pull her in contrary directions. She often felt great irritation at her coworkers, including Cady Stanton, who would persist in having children. "Now Nettie," she warned Antoinette Brown Blackwell, congratulating her on the birth of her second daughter, "*not another baby . . . two* will solve the problem whether a *woman can* be anything more than a *wife* and *mother* better than a half dozen." While women with young children felt frustrated that they could not work more effectively for the cause because of domestic duties, those duties may also have provided a respite from the incessant demands of Anthony and the movement—a period of necessary withdrawal. "As soon as you all begin to ask too much of me, I shall have a baby!" warned Cady Stanton—perhaps only half in jest—to one of Anthony's insistent requests.

The difficulty of finding women with time to dedicate to the movement was compounded by the problem of money. Even shoestring operations need funds. Running conventions, publishing proceedings, printing petitions all required cash. And the women who traveled as lecturers for the cause could not be expected to absorb all their expenses, especially those who, like Anthony and Lucy Stone before her marriage, essentially earned their living by lecturing and reform work. Organizers used various expedients to get a working budget. Lecturers ordinarily charged an entrance fee or passed the hat at the end of the session. The standard convention fee was twenty-five cents per day. Occasionally a well-wisher would give one of the leaders ten or twenty dollars, and the wealthy Gerrit Smith made significant donations until 1856, when he diverted his help to John Brown. Finances were handled quite casually: the treasurer (who was often Anthony) disbursed the funds according to his or her good sense and on the advice of a few others, because, as Antoinette Brown said, "we have all believed in and trusted each other."

In 1858–1859 financial pressures were eased by a couple of windfalls. The wealthy abolitionist and feminist Francis Jackson gave $5,000 to be used for women's rights activities. Since there was no society to which the money could be given, it was put under the trusteeship of Wendell Phillips, Susan B. Anthony, and Lucy Stone to dispense. The following year Charles F. Hovey, another wealthy reformer, left an endowment of $50,000, the income to be split between antislavery and women's rights.

Inevitably those who faithfully attended conventions year after year began to complain they were hearing the same people say much the same thing they had heard many times before. Many were becoming restless at the repetition of what Gerrit Smith in 1855 dismissed as "righteous demands and noble sentiments," and there were increasing calls for action, not just words. In fact actions were being taken, with varying degrees of success. Ongoing campaigns in various states sought new or expanded married women's property laws. New York was the site of a major effort by Ernestine Rose and Susan Anthony to extend the 1848 law to cover wages as well as inheritances, and to give mothers joint legal custody of children. In 1854 Anthony organized an extensive petition campaign, sending teams of women door to door, in midwinter, to gather signatures. She also organized a convention to take place in Albany while the legislature was in session; large audiences, including many state representatives, attended its evening lectures. Elizabeth Cady Stanton delivered a long speech to the Joint Judiciary Committee, and Anthony had the address printed and distributed to every member of the legislature. But the select committee that considered the petitions rejected the idea of the legal equality of husband and wife, deciding that "a higher power than that from which emanates legislative enactments has given forth the mandate that man and woman shall not be equal."

Determined to maintain the pressure in New York, Anthony and a team of speakers canvassed the state every year until by 1860 the opposition seemed to be weakening. Cady

Stanton addressed a joint session of the legislature in March, and the following day a law passed granting married women in New York control of their own earnings and joint legal guardianship of their children with their husbands. As with the earlier property laws, other legal and political interests helped pass the legislation, but the dogged persistence of the women over six years was clearly a major factor in achieving success.

Similar campaigns took place in other states. While not always successful, they had important benefits for the movement. They elicited support from women and men who might have recoiled from a blanket assertion of equality but were prepared for piecemeal reform. They also created a cadre of local leaders and gave the movement presence in the political arena. While the American federal system was a disadvantage in the sense that it required the waging of separate battles in each state, it also allowed plenty of scope for local leadership to emerge, and these campaigns provided a focus for the growth of local women's movements. Every practical success was also a boost for morale. Lucy Stone reported jubilantly to Anthony in 1856 that the state of Ohio had passed laws on property and child custody, giving "to wives equal property rights, and to mothers, equal baby rights." "The world moves!" she exulted. "Hurrah!"

From time to time suggestions were heard for a more concrete organization, but the sense of the majority was against the move. A motion to organize a National Women's Rights Society prompted a spirited discussion at the 1852 national convention in Syracuse. But Angelina Grimké had sent a letter vigorously pointing out that the tendency of organizations "is to sink the individual in the mass. . . . What organization in the world's history has not encumbered the unfettered action of those who created it?" Lucy Stone and Ernestine Rose concurred, and the motion was defeated. By 1859, however, there was growing pressure for tighter central organization. Antoinette Brown Blackwell thought the movement had reached a point of maturity where it needed a clear-cut national society, "a real entity . . . to do business decently and in order." No action was taken at the 1859 meeting, but a new systematization was evident. On Blackwell's suggestion, a committee was named to draw up uniform memorials asking for full legal equal rights for women, to be delivered to every state legislature in the Northern states.

The political debate over the extension of slavery had been gathering momentum since the mid-1850s, and many women's rights advocates were now increasingly preoccupied with national politics. In the gathering crisis, antislavery loomed as large a concern for many feminists as the women's cause. In January 1861 Anthony organized a tour of antislavery speakers, including Elizabeth Cady Stanton, Lucretia Mott, and Frederick Douglass among others, through upstate New York, designed to pressure President-elect Lincoln into taking a stand on the abolition of slavery. Public fears about the dissolution of the union were now at fever pitch, and in several places the speakers were mobbed. "Won't Susan enjoy it?" remarked Lucy Stone wickedly.

By mid-April 1861 the nation was at war. A national women's rights convention had been scheduled for May. Blackwell, on the roster to speak, hastily changed her topic to "The Relation of the Woman Question to Our National Crisis," but the organizers decided to cancel the convention altogether. Over the objections of Susan B. Anthony, but with the concurrence of the other leaders, agitation for women's rights would be put on hold for the duration of the war.

4

Diagnosing the Problem:
What Did Women Want?

Who are these women? what do they want? what are the motives that impel them to this course of action?—*New York Herald*, September 12, 1852

THE WOMEN'S MOVEMENT took root in its early years in the same regions that had already been thoroughly seeded with reform ideas and organizations: upstate New York, Massachusetts, parts of Pennsylvania, and the Ohio Western Reserve. The most fertile soil proved to be in small towns, especially those on growing transport networks, with a variety of businesses, some professionals, and a newspaper. These were the kinds of communities that Susan B. Anthony characterized as "wide awake." Here could be found whole families, kin and friendship groups, who provided the networks through which women's rights ideas could travel and which would provide both leaders and core followers. Existing reform communities of various kinds provided recruiting grounds for both leaders and followers: antislavery societies, Temperance groups, the spiritualist and health reform movements, the groups of radical Quakers who called themselves

"Progressive Friends," and the experiments in communal living that dotted these same areas in the 1840s and 1850s.

In the South there was no women's movement. Feminism,
like most other "isms" of the day, did not penetrate below the
Mason-Dixon line—a fact that Southerners took as a mark of
their superior civilization. Whatever private discontent
Southern women may have felt, they had no way of articulat-
ing it as a public issue. In its personnel, its ideology, and its
methods, the women's movement was allied in the Southern
mind with the abolition of slavery, which made it automatically taboo in a region that had closed its gates in defense of
the institution.

In its rank and file and its leadership, the women's rights
movement was thoroughly middle class. It arose from the
same class that was contemporaneously involved in abolition,
Temperance, prison reform, and the other progressive movements of the day, and that has produced the leadership of most
of the reform, revolutionary, and anticolonial movements of
the nineteenth and twentieth centuries. The movement won
no recruits among very wealthy women, and in spite of the endorsement of Seneca Falls by *The Factory Girl's Voice* in 1848,
there was little involvement by wage-earning or working-
class women, nor by representatives of the large-scale Irish
and Catholic immigration that began in the late 1840s.

As the sociologist Steven Buechler has pointed out, it is a
central characteristic of liberal middle-class and white movements that they tend to be oblivious to their own class and
racial character, and see themselves and their demands as
"universal." Certainly the leaders of the women's movement
claimed they spoke for "all" women. Such an assumption may
repel other classes and races, who may find the movement's
ideology and goals less than relevant to their own situation,
and its "style" off-putting.

Middle-class black women did attend conventions and occasionally spoke from the floor, and the antislavery lecturer Sarah Remond spoke from the platform in 1858, but no black women seem to have held office in the women's movement. The relative invisibility of middle-class black women in the movement before the Civil War is striking in view of the quite prominent role taken by black men. Frederick Douglass was a major figure who spoke frequently, and Robert Purvis, the wealthy black Philadelphian, was a regular participant at conventions and served several times as a vice-president.

It may be that African-American women were so strongly involved in antislavery and self-help organizations in the black community that in those contexts they were enacting their own emancipation, both racially and sexually. Certainly women made a strong bid for the right to speak and participate in the major African-American political organization of the antebellum period, the Black Convention Movement. As early as 1848 an African-American woman at one of these conventions asserted that women should be included in the demand for the franchise. While there was some resistance to this idea, on the whole organized black men seem to have been rather more open to the equal participation of women than most white men.

A major exception to the relative invisibility of African-American women in the movement at this point was the towering figure of Sojourner Truth. A woman of striking appearance (she was six feet tall), she had led an extraordinary life. Born a slave in New York state in 1797 and emancipated by the state law of 1827, she took the name of Sojourner Truth after a religious experience. By the 1850s she had become a frequent and well-known antislavery speaker. She was illiterate, but as she told the Stanton children who tried to teach her to read, "I read men."

Sojourner Truth had been present at the Rochester convention in 1848 and had made a decisive intervention at the Akron, Ohio, convention of 1851. In response to several stern rebukes from clergymen present, she delivered an electrifying speech that has become one of the icons of feminist history, in the version as embellished and written down many years later by Frances Gage. Taking on the oft-heard defense of the status quo that women were too weak and delicate for the rough and tumble of the world outside the home, she recounted her hardships under slavery, and the physical labor she had performed as well as men. It was apparently a masterly piece of oratory and a vivid demonstration of the *strength* of a woman's body as well as her spirit. After this sensational debut, Sojourner Truth remained a prominent figure in the women's movement.

All the women who launched the movement came out of the general reform milieu, especially antislavery and Temperance. Their fathers and husbands tended to be professionals or in some kind of business. Most were born between 1805 and 1825. Lucretia Mott, the eldest, was born in 1793 and so was fifty-five at the Seneca Falls meeting. The youngest were Caroline Dall and Antoinette Brown, born in 1822 and 1825 respectively. An unusually large number had been self-supporting for some part of their lives. Lucy Stone and Susan B. Anthony had been teachers and paid antislavery agents; Stone, Paulina Wright Davis, and Elizabeth Jones were successful freelance lecturers, as was Antoinette Brown. Frances Gage and Clarina Wright Nichols were newspaper journalists and editors; Elizabeth Oakes Smith was a successful writer; Ernestine Rose was an inventor and businesswoman. After her minister husband virtually abandoned her to become a missionary, Caroline Dall partially supported herself and her children through writing. Elizabeth Cady Stanton was always comfortably off, and none of them had known absolute poverty. But Anthony, Nichols, Stone, and Dall, at least, had experienced periods of economic stringency. Lucy Stone had had to work and save for nine years in order to pay her way through Oberlin. Like many middle-class women of the period, they knew that life was uncertain and that there was no guarantee they would always enjoy the comforts of a middle-class home.

With the exception of Ernestine Rose, they were all native born. The only other prominent immigrant in the movement was Mathilde Anneke, a leader in Wisconsin. Both these women were radicals when they arrived in America. Except for these two, all the women were Protestant, but they were either born into, or moved into, affiliation with liberal congregations, such as Quakers, Unitarians, and Universalists. Davis became a spiritualist, Hunt a Swedenborgian. Adhesion to any church that emphasized authority, either of a hierarchy or of the Bible, was incompatible with feminism. Antoinette Brown, who was actually called as a Congregationalist minister, lasted in her congregation only a year before she began to have doubts. She became a Unitarian.

Most of the leaders married, though they tended to marry later than the norm for the period. Rose, Davis, and Bloomer were childless, but the others had children, ranging in number from Frances Gage's eight and Cady Stanton's seven to Stone's one. Whatever the size of their families, all had fewer children than their own mothers had had. Nichols and sometime sympathizer Jane Smisshelm were divorced, but others, like Mott and Antoinette Brown Blackwell, seem to have had conspicuously happy marriages.

The standard of education for the group as a whole was above the average for American women, even of the middle class. Two, Stone and Blackwell, were college graduates. Even those, like Frances Gage, whose formal education was meager, educated themselves through wide reading. Indeed, most of the leaders seem to have been lifelong readers who tried to keep up with the intellectual currents of the day. In their letters, Blackwell, Cady Stanton, Anthony, and Stone all speak of reading Emerson, Herbert Spencer, Darwin, and John Stuart Mill; Stanton read Comte. They read imaginative literature too. Everyone appears to have read *Uncle Tom's Cabin*, but the works that seem to have had the most resonance for them were Elizabeth Barrett Browning's feminist narrative poem "Aurora Leigh," Charlotte Bronte's *Jane Eyre*, and the novels of George Eliot. They read always with an eye to the import of the work for the position of women.

Male feminists came from the same class background, the same liberal religion, and the same general reform connections as the women. Their general level of formal education and professional involvement was higher than the women's. Some were husbands of women in the movement, but most allied themselves to it independently of their wives. They seem to have come to the movement out of a strong ideological commitment to principles of freedom and individual equality that was part of their baptism in antislavery.

Besides their general class and race composition, there is one other striking characteristic of many feminist women: their affinity for various nineteenth-century "New Age" movements. Many were impressed by phrenology, the new "science" that appeared to offer insight into reading human character by studying the contours of the head. Others were attracted to various utopian communities, such as Hopedale in Massachusetts, Skaneatles in New York, or the Raritan Bay Union in New Jersey, where Weld and the Grimké sisters opened an experimental boarding school.

Many women's rights advocates were also drawn to spiritualism, the fast-growing religious movement that swept through the same regions as antislavery and women's rights in mid-century. Spiritualists abandoned churchly organization, creeds, and an authoritative ministry in favor of individual contact with spiritual reality through the channel of a medium, who was more often than not a woman. Spiritualists also supported most of the progressive reforms of the day, including the equality of women.

As in the late-twentieth-century women's movement, a strong concern with woman's health, coupled with an equally strong distrust of the male medical establishment, was apparent among nineteenth-century feminists. Members of the women's movement were particularly drawn to various popular unorthodox therapies such as the "water cure," homeopathy, or healthy diets based on pure water, grains, and vegetables. These offered the prospect that women could regain control of their own health care and that of their families. The mainstream medical profession was extremely hostile to the entrance of women. Elizabeth Blackwell's acceptance and graduation from Geneva Medical College in 1849 was not followed by a general opening of medical schools to women. The various "irregular" schools of medicine were much more accepting, however, and almost all the small number of women who practiced medicine before the Civil War had been trained in one of the alternative schools, such as the Female Medical College of Philadelphia, founded in 1850. In addition, a number of women in the 1840s, including major feminist Paulina Wright (Davis) and fringe feminist Mary Gove Nichols, had started to lecture to women's groups on physiology, convinced that women's emancipation depended on their being able to understand the workings of their own bodies and the "laws" of health.

What might be called a new "woman's" attitude toward
health can be clearly seen in the career and writings of feminist Harriot Hunt. A New Englander born in 1805, Hunt
taught herself medicine from books and observation. Since
there was in these early years no state licensing system in operation, she was able to set up what became an extremely successful practice in Boston, treating women and children.
When she had been practicing for several years, she applied
twice to Harvard Medical School and was refused admission.

Hunt's medical philosophy advocated prevention over cure.
She urged women to learn about their own bodies, so that to a
considerable extent they would be able to dispense with physicians. She deplored what she saw as the overintrusive, over-
medicating, and authoritarian approach of the male medical
establishment. She tried to probe for the psychological roots of
her patients' maladies in the unhappiness and frustration of
their lives. Above all, she thought that medicine must be a
partnership between doctor, patient, and the patient's family
who, nursing the patient from day to day, might well have
more acute observations about how the disease was progress-
ing than the doctor. The popular movements in medicine
were already seeking an alternative to the authoritarian model
of godlike physician and obedient subject. "The public are
getting enlightened," she warned the medical profession, "and
you must recognize it. . . . The day of blind obedience, or foolish deference, to you is entirely gone."

Factors such as class, religion, ethnicity, and affinity for
other kinds of radical reform movements may be shared characteristics, but they are not in themselves explanatory. After
all, most middle-class, white, Protestant women and men living in the Northeast did *not* attach themselves to the women's
movement. Feminism arose within the broad middle classes,

but most middle-class people were opposed to it. What, then, motivated these particular women to challenge the powerful gender norms of their society?

Emily Collins's story offers clues about motivation. In her reminiscences, Collins offered two reasons for her conversion to women's rights. The first was personal, her feeling of being unjustly deprived of opportunity for growth; the second was her witnessing of an oppression that she did not personally suffer—a neighboring woman who was regularly beaten by her husband, a leader in the Methodist church. These appear to have been the twin motivations of most women who became part of the movement. Few women seem to have become feminists because they had personally experienced actual physical violence and abuse from husbands—though some had certainly experienced the economic hardship that the death or business failure of a spouse, or his abandonment of her, could bring to an unprepared wife. But the *existence* of such abuse does seem to have been a powerful factor in producing women's anger. The narratives at conventions, or in letters and articles in the women's press, are filled with stories of abused women, often introduced as personal knowledge: "I know a woman who . . ." Their response to this knowledge was not just pity but outrage and humiliation that such things could be done to people like themselves. "Individually," admitted Paulina Wright Davis, in the first issue of the *Una*, they had suffered few wrongs, "but in our human sympathies, we have suffered from every infliction upon the dependent class to which we belong."

Feminism seems to have appealed most powerfully to women who felt personally the wrongs inflicted on others, or to women whose own aspirations had been thwarted. Having talents and desires for a wider life that were denied purely because of their sex left a lasting bitterness. The language of

WHAT DID WOMEN WANT?

feminism in these years is replete with adjectives such as "crushed," "confined," "crippled." Few stated the feeling more poignantly than the middle-aged woman who spoke from the floor at the Worcester convention, recounting her never-forgotten resentment as a girl that she could not get the education available to her brothers. "I wanted to be what I felt that I was capable of becoming," she said, but that possibility had been forever closed off because of her sex. Being shut out from opportunities for self-development inflicted a loss that could never be recouped. "If we do not properly develop our human natures in this sphere of existence," declared Abby Price of the Hopedale Community at the 1850 Worcester convention, "it is a loss that can never be made up," for "development constitutes our *greatness* and our *happiness*." These two strands—women's wrongs and women's rights, the discourse of complaint and the discourse of aspiration—remained interwoven throughout the history of the women's movement.

Feminists were acutely aware of belonging to an inferior caste, excluded by law and public opinion from most worthwhile fields of human endeavor on grounds of incompetency. The language of the common law, the phrases in common use, all drove home society's low estimate and low expectations of women. The modern feminist keyword "oppression" was not used much in nineteenth-century feminist discourse. Rather, the word that turns up again and again is "degradation." Oppression connotes suffering, but degradation implies shame, indignity. What these early feminist leaders felt was *humiliation*. As a spur to revolt, humiliation is probably a sharper and more effective goad than material oppression.

Cady Stanton seems to have felt the humiliation of women's status acutely. While the analogy between woman and slave was fairly commonplace, Cady Stanton was unusual in pointing to the congruence of sexism with the racism experienced

by the free African-American population. She felt a sympathetic identification with people like Frederick Douglass, or
the wealthy, cultivated Robert Purvis, who with all the attri-
butes of individual superiority were constantly subjected to the
indignities of racial prejudice. The "humiliation of color" and
the humiliation of sex, she thought, were analogous. "To the
white man the world throws open its gates—all your efforts
are praised and encouraged," she told a committee of the New
York legislature, "all your successes are welcomed with loud
hurrahs and cheers; but the black man and the woman are
born to shame. The badge of degradation is the skin and sex."

To purge their humiliation, women needed to assert their
equality, and equality necessitated dismantling the doctrine of
"separate spheres." Feminists had no illusions about what separate spheres meant in practice; it meant exclusion and inferiority. What distinguished feminists from other women
activists was that they were not interested in expanding
women's sphere, or exalting its value; they wished to break
down its walls.

Caroline Dall summed up the goals of the movement as
they had crystallized by 1860: "First, Absolute freedom in education; absolute, unquestioned access to all public institutions, to all libraries and museums, to all means of
culture,—artistic, aesthetic, scientific, or professional.

"Second, Absolute freedom of vocation; and this freedom
involves such a change in public thinking as shall make it honorable for all women to work, not merely for bread, for the
support of husband or child, but for fame, for money, for
work's own sake, as men work.

"Third, equality before the law, which, of course, involves
the right of suffrage."

In short, equal rights of access as individuals, equal rights of
participation as citizens, and the removal of all legal disabili-

ties. These goals were predicated upon two basic values which lay at the heart of the feminist model for a new womanhood: self-development and independence.

As Dall indicated, self-development depended on education. Feminists were not content with the special all-female institutions built up and advocated by women like Beecher and Willard. They suspected that these would always be essentially inferior to the best men's colleges. Self-development meant access on the same terms as men to the best available means of education and to the whole range of civilized achievement. Feminists always linked education to some use in the world beyond self-culture. Wendell Phillips ridiculed reformers who wanted to give women higher education and then expected her to use it purely in the family circle. "Educate her in science, that she may go home and take care of her cradle! Teach her . . . political economy, that she may smile sweetly when her husband comes home!" The educated woman, he maintained, needed just what men needed, the stimulus of "the world's honors, its gold, and its fame."

Thus there was a natural feminist progression from education to work. Work, indeed, held a central place in feminist ideology, for it was the key to independence. The meaning of independence for feminists was not much different from what it was in traditional republican ideology as adapted to the conditions of a modern capitalist economy. The model republican citizen was the "independent" man, the man whose integrity of character rested on the solid material base of being able to support himself decently. In appropriating this ideal for women, feminists were attacking head-on the central point of the separate spheres ideology: that woman was naturally dependent on man.

Independence was a characterological as well as a material ideal. Cady Stanton in particular always insisted that it in-

volved the strength of the body, which in turn affected the
self-reliance of the mind. She had been an athletic young
woman and was a tireless advocate of exercise and physical activity for girls. "The girl must be allowed to romp and play,
climb, skate, and swim," she insisted. This childhood freedom
would allow her to grow up a strong and healthy woman, af-
fording her both self-confidence and the essential virile virtue
of courage. Girls were not only socialized to be physically
weak, she complained, they were also socialized to be timid
and to entertain fears beyond actual dangers. In a letter to the
Akron convention of 1851, Cady Stanton urged parents to
teach their daughters to be bold and brave. "Teach her to go
alone," she wrote, "by night and day, if need be, on the lonely
highway, or through the busy streets of the crowded metropo-
lis. . . . Better, far, suffer occasional insults, or die outright,
than live the life of a *coward*, or never move without a protector. The best protector that any woman can have, one that will
serve her at all times and in all places, is *courage*; this she must
get by her own experience; and experience comes by exposure."

Essentially, though, the capacity to be independent in the
modern world meant the ability to earn one's own living in
the marketplace. This was something few women did or
would be able to do with ease, for the wages paid to women
were notoriously low. This was partly due, feminists thought,
to gender discrimination. Women's work was devalued because women were devalued. Tailoresses, for example, were
always paid considerably less than tailors, not because of the
quality of their work but because of their gender.

Feminists also accepted the more generally held market explanation. Women were paid so little because they were kept
out of most jobs and so drove down the wages of those they
flooded into. The major line of work for women was domestic

service, followed by the textile industry, shoe-binding, hat-making, teaching, and hand-sewing. For many reformers, sewing women, stitching shirts from dawn to dusk at sixty cents a dozen, became a popular symbol of the heartlessness of the modern capitalist economy. The popularity of the exploited seamstress symbol, however, owed much to its ambiguity. Many of the sewing women were deserted wives or widows, or women with disabled husbands. Their pitiable state was an object lesson in what happened to women on their own. Expanding work opportunities for women like this attracted support from many quarters since it was, within limits, the kind of practical reform that could be supported without challenging male supremacy. The *New York Tribune*, for example, heartily endorsed the creation of a school of design for women: "here is a plan to help women which does not involve any vexed question respecting Woman's Rights."

To feminists, the sewing woman, like the prostitute, was the awful fate that women must protect themselves against by acquiring marketable skills. A mother of five daughters wrote to the *Una* in 1853 that she hoped to educate them all to a trade. Why should they not be florists, farmers, cabinetmakers, upholsterers, lawyers, doctors, or preachers? Anything "to save them from stitching from early morn til late at night." Convention speakers urged women to explore options like design, or applied fine arts such as the painting of china. They advocated dentistry, the new craft of photography, work as a saleswoman, or as a clerk in business or government offices, or as a telegraph operator; even factory work was acceptable as long as it paid decently. They particularly recommended printing, one of the best-paid and most middle class of craft jobs. They did not recommend domestic service.

Work that required skill had a moral dimension; it gave discipline to character and would give women a "project" of their own in life. But it was the money provided by work that was its essential value, because money was the foundation of independence. "Poverty," Paulina Wright Davis told her readers in the *Una*, "is essentially slavery, if not legal, yet actual."

> The women of the time—the women worthy of the time—must understand this, and they must *go to work*. They must press into every avenue, every open door, that custom and law leave unguarded, aye, and themselves withdraw the bolts and bars from others still closed against them, that they may enter and take possession. . . . In a word we must buy ourselves out of bondage, and work our way into liberty and honor. For just as long as the world stands, its government will go with its cares, services and responsibilities. Children and women, til they can keep themselves, will be kept in pupilage by the same power which supports them.

The 1851 Worcester convention endorsed the resolution that every woman interested in women's rights "should seek out as speedily as possible some legitimate way of getting money."

Davis was concerned not just that women should be able to make a living but that well-educated and energetic women should be able to make a career in the professions or "the higher functions of business." It was one of the principal sins of man, according to the Seneca Falls declaration, that he had closed against woman "all the avenues to wealth and distinction which he considers most honorable to himself." Feminists wanted to be able to follow those avenues to wealth and distinction. Over and over they cited examples of women who had achieved distinction in the male world of work—Rosa Bonheur, the artist; Harriet Hosmer, the American sculptor; the businesswoman who had built the largest china business in the country; another who had developed the largest shoe store; Elizabeth Blackwell; Florence Nightingale.

It was one thing to exhort women to break into new kinds

of work; it was quite another to stimulate a response. It was often pointed out that there were no actual laws preventing women from entering most lines of work; what prevented them was their own diffidence about their capabilities, fear of public opinion, or unwillingness to acquire marketable skills or take on responsibilities. Too many young women just assumed they would marry and be taken care of for the rest of their lives, and too many mothers insisted this was the only proper course. "I know girls who have mechanical genius," said one speaker at a convention, but their mothers would not allow them to apprentice in a mechanical trade. "Which of the women at this Convention," she challenged, "have sent their daughters as apprentices to a watchmaker?" Lucy Stone pointed out that it was not just a question of female will; there was often the determined opposition of male workers to contend with. The few women who were trying to break into printing, for example, usually could not get far in the trade because skilled male printers refused to teach them. Often they were fired because men threatened to strike rather than work with women.

Feminists such as Davis, Dall, and Angelina Grimké thought it desirable that women continue to work after marriage, since only thus could they retain real independence. Most feminists, however, regarded a marketable skill as desirable chiefly for young women, so they could avoid the humiliation of having to marry someone they did not love because it was the only way they could be certain of a decent living. For a married woman a marketable skill would be a useful resource in case of economic problems, widowhood, or desertion. Most discussions assumed that in marriages that included children, the wife and mother fully earned her living by her child-rearing and domestic work. Far from despising the housewife's work, feminists insisted that she earned her keep. Rose pointed out that property acquired during a marriage was usually the result of the joint labors of man and wife, even if only the man supplied the cash, and should be recognized as such by law. At the same time most feminists felt that a woman with a particular "calling" should be able to combine it with marriage.

The greater availability of household help and more extended networks of family who could share child-minding probably made life easier for a nineteenth-century career woman than for her twentieth-century counterpart. Much professional work, such as medicine, could be performed from the home, and the kind of business career envisaged entailed individual entrepreneurship, not dedication of all waking hours to the service of the corporation.

An interesting letter on the question of combining work with marriage was written by a young woman, Olympia Brown, to Antoinette Brown Blackwell (no relation). Olympia was an early student at Antioch College and intended to become a minister, but she also wished to marry and have children. She admired Blackwell as a pioneer in both regards. In 1861 she wrote to the older woman asking how she had managed it. In reply, Blackwell acknowledged that the mother of a young family could not absorb herself wholly in her profession, but she could adapt her work to her life cycle: marry at twenty-five to thirty, advised Blackwell, after having begun a profession; for the next twenty years combine part-time professional work with child-rearing, then devote the next twenty years, "the prime of life," entirely to the chosen work. Ideally, however, women must eventually be able to "bend the professions to themselves and their capacities," and men and women both should adopt the motto: "the professions are made for man, not man for the professions." Blackwell hoped the time would come when men too would be "more than professional drudges and business machines," and husbands and wives would share and cooperate in the work of the family and the work of the world. Until that time, she acknowledged, women who "take marked public positions must be in some sense exceptional persons. All leaders in every new movement are such."

The feminist emphasis on self-development and independence placed them in the mainstream of early-nineteenth-century romantic individualism, which also enabled them to avoid a number of intellectual problems. They could just dismiss the whole question of *woman's* proper sphere, for example. They insisted repeatedly that each individual had his or her own "proper" sphere, and that was "the largest and highest to which they are able to attain," as the 1851 Worcester convention resolved. Certainly no one had the right to define a "sphere" for anyone else. The notion of the individual that emerges from feminist writing and rhetoric is not an enclosed competitive atom, guarding his rights against all comers, but a creature of needs and wants, a bundle of potentialities that craved and deserved the opportunity for realization. "The fundamental principle of the Woman's Rights movement," resolved an 1853 convention, "is . . . that every human being, without distinction of sex, has an inviolable right to the full development and free exercise of all energies."

Individualism also enabled feminists to dodge such sticky problems as the relative abilities of men and women and the question of gender "difference." Whether "man" and "woman" had equal or unequal capacities was literally meaningless, for a talent or capacity was a property of the individual, not of the group to which that person belonged or was assigned. The question of the likeness or unlikeness of the sexes seems to be an endemic philosophical preoccupation in all phases of women's movements. Philosophic disputes over "difference" were not absent in these early stages, but on the whole the weight of feminist thinking was on the side of emphasizing the common humanity and thus common title to liberty and the rights of men and women, rather than any essential womanly character.

Feminists were not rebelling against being women, but "woman" was after all a category which had been clamped upon them and which they experienced as confining and deforming. They were more likely to perceive each human being as an individual with a number of different characteristics, one of which was gender. In some circumstances that characteristic was central; in others it was or ought to be irrelevant. Both Cady Stanton and Anthony believed strongly in coeducation and thought differences of sex to be irrelevant in the classroom. Thomas Wentworth Higginson offered a graphic illustration. While the distinction of sex certainly ran throughout nature, still, "the eagle is not checked in soaring by any consciousness of sex," he pointed out, "nor asks the sex of the timid hare, its quarry." In this situation, the operative distinction was not between male and female but between hunter and hunted.

Cady Stanton substantially modified her stand on the "difference" question later in her career, but before the Civil War she was quite unequivocal that all the talk of essential differences between men and women was "mysterious 'twaddle.'" She saw the dangers for women's emancipation in "difference" arguments. "Admit a radical difference in sex," she warned, "and you demand different spheres." "Difference" would soon be run into "the old groove of superiority." She thought, moreover, that tyranny and inhumanity arose from mankind's propensity for believing people of other groups to be so radically different from themselves that empathy was impossible; people could not imagine themselves in another person's place. Whites could enslave Africans, in spite of a general philosophy that valued freedom, because they did not believe that Africans felt loss of freedom exactly as they would themselves. Similarly, men denied women opportunity because they did not think that women resented it as they themselves would. The problem, she told the New York legislature, was that men "cannot take in the idea that men and women are alike."

On the other hand, the pull of "difference," so central to the entire culture, was not without power in the movement. Paulina Davis and Lucretia Mott always sharply denied that women had any moral superiority to men, but the notion obviously had considerable charm. Perhaps gender difference resonated more strongly in the experience of most women than among the leadership. In 1858 Eliza Farnham, who had once crossed swords with John Neal, turned up at the national convention in New York. She had now been converted to women's rights, but on the basis that women were both biologically and spiritually superior to men. Her message to the convention was that the new higher era that was dawning would show women in the ascendant (an idea she expounded at length in her 1864 book *Woman and Her Era*). Among the leaders on the platform there was some discomfort with this. They protested they would be quite content with equality. But Farnham's speech, according to the report, was received with "apparent satisfaction by the audience." The leadership may not have been in tune with the rank and file on this question.

In any case, whether the female individual was like or unlike the male individual, inferior or superior to him, was irrelevant to the fundamental fact that she was by nature a rights bearer. Both her self-respect and her ability to fulfill her potential demanded that she have equal rights with man in all

departments of life. The language of rights came naturally to
American women because in Western culture the language of
rights has been not only the language of defense and protection but the language of empowerment. Translating aspirations for a different and more satisfying life into demands for
rights created culturally understood claims for dignity and
consideration. A demand for rights might be rejected, but the
position gave the claimant a standing, in her own eyes and
others', above that of the petitioner.

Nineteenth-century feminists never doubted that the individual was first and foremost a moral being, nor did they ever
deny the reality of community obligations or of binding personal ties. The problem for women was that both public opinion and the law saw them *only* as part of a network of
relations, with no intrinsic worth or even existence outside of
them. A woman was essentially either a wife or a potential
wife, and therefore always "supported" by someone else. Thus
she did not need access to well-paying work. She was a citizen,
but a subordinate one who was always represented by someone else, so she did not need a vote. She was a mother whose
claim to education or to prestige rested on her role in child-
rearing. She was a creature intended by nature to live for and
through others, so she needed no outlet for her talents or ambitions except the opportunity to nurture those of her husband
and sons.

Since all human beings were alike in having physical and
emotional needs, moral obligations, and intellectual capacities,
even though the nature and extent of these might vary among
individuals and in different circumstances, feminists insisted
that rights must by their nature be equal and universal. Equality of rights in no way depended on equality or identity of capacity, insisted Abby Price. It was only necessary to maintain
that all human beings are "absolutely equal in their rights to

life, liberty and the pursuit of happiness—in their rights *to do* and *to be, individually* and *socially*, all they are capable of, and to attain the highest usefulness and happiness, obediently to the *divine moral law*." Indeed, feminists often said they were demanding not women's rights but *human* rights.

The early-nineteenth-century feminists did not conceive of rights as created by government and positive law, nor as merely static claims against the encroachments of others. A revival of natural law theory was current among abolitionists and was equally attractive to the women's movement. The concept of rights elaborated in the speeches and writings of the movement saw them as derived essentially from human nature, from human needs, wants, and capabilities. As the writer calling herself an "Indignant Factory Girl" had insisted to the *Voice of Industry* in 1847, "So far as [woman] can create a new field of endeavor and hope, she has new rights." The underlying fundamental of all rights "is summed up in one word, the right to be whole." The title given to a series of tracts on women's rights, published in 1853, echoed these ideas: *Woman's Rights Commensurate with Her Capacities and Obligations.*

Because feminists emphasized the human potential for growth and development, their concept of rights was dynamic rather than static. Not only did the recognition and claim to rights unfold progressively throughout history, but the development of civilization increased both human wants and human capacities; thus the rights necessary to use and meet them were equally subject to expansion. "I am a disciple of the new philosophy that man's wants make his rights," wrote Cady Stanton to Anthony in 1858. Ernestine Rose agreed: rights sprang from wants, she told the 1854 Cleveland convention. Rights in turn gave rise to duties, and "the more rights we enjoy, the greater the duties we owe." The current problem was that men enjoyed all the rights but "preached duty to women."

Of all the equal rights women demanded, the most contentious was the right to vote. They assumed this would also entail the right to serve on juries and the right to hold political office. The vote was not as central to feminist demands at this time as it later became. But it was viewed as a necessary part of the total package of women's emancipation, for to be excluded from the central ritual of the nation was to be deprived of that recognition necessary for feeling like a free person. As Caroline Dall put it in 1855, "The right of suffrage has a two-fold meaning. It expresses power, and it expresses the respect in which that power is held. Men will not respect women as they should, until they confer upon them this right, or what amounts to the same thing, they will not confer it on her until they respect her more than they do now. They will not educate her, pay her, protect her property, until she is herself a power in the Commonwealth." The Ohio leader Caroline Severance saw the vote rather as a means of educating women into greater self-respect. "In no other way," she told an 1853 Ohio convention, could woman be so surely aroused to "the recognition of her individual worth and responsibility, her independent selfhood, as by securing for her the rights of citizenship, the privileges of freemen."

The historian Ellen DuBois has argued that the vote was the most radical of all the women's demands, because it decisively bridged the divide between the public and private worlds, the male and female spheres. One woman, one vote recognized a woman as a freestanding citizen, outside of family relationships. It would also mark the ultimate demise of coverture, since women's inclusion in the Republic would no longer be as part of the domestic hinterland of the male citizen but in her own proper person. She would represent herself.

In representing herself, feminists hoped, she would also transform herself. The most important target audience for the women's rights movement was not men, or even male legislators, it was women themselves. It was women who needed to be both aroused and reformed. Feminists not only wanted women to live in different circumstances, they wanted them to be different kinds of people. They were humiliated not only by the strictures on their sex but by the character of many other women. This was at the heart of their frequent comparison between the situation of the married free woman and the slave. Feminists had picked up from the abolitionists a critique of slavery that located its worst oppression less in its physical cruelty than in its deformation of personality. To live totally under the control of another man's will, bent entirely to another man's purposes, deprived the victims of energy and enterprise and forced them to become devious, cunning, and servile. Publicists of separate spheres attributed women's greater purity and elevation of character to her domestic dependence, but feminists insisted that it was more likely to produce a character type lacking in integrity, courage, and generosity.

Speakers and writers were not afraid to spell out the effects of patriarchy on the character of women. Epithets such as "weak," "meager," "inconstant," "inefficient," "petulant," "treacherous," "petty," "servile," and "devious" were freely used. Caroline Dall, reflecting on the low public estimate of women throughout the ages, admitted that considering the historical socialization of women, "it does not seem strange, that, after ages passed in a false position, she should somewhat approximate to this estimate; so that we say with pain of the mass of women, that *they themselves* need a change quite as much as their circumstances."

To feminists, of course, nothing demonstrated more clearly

the infantilizing and debasing effect of the patriarchal regime on women's character than all the women who said complacently, "We have all the rights we want!" The more optimistic, such as Dall, thought that all over the country there were women who were "dimly conscious that they are not all they ought to be" and thus had "a secret, undefined sympathy" for any move benefiting women. She thought they would like to aid the movement as long as they could do so without going to conventions, making speeches, or wearing peculiar clothes. For them the barrier was not the specific goals of the movement but the reluctance to challenge head-on their husbands, their ministers, and public opinion, and risk their incomprehension, their anger, and perhaps most of all their ridicule. But the accuracy of this appraisal is impossible to test. Over and over again, women's rights advocates had to admit that it was less men than women themselves who blocked the progress of their cause, and they deplored the apathy and even the downright hostility they found among women. "The most discouraging, the most lamentable aspect our cause wears," admitted Cady Stanton in 1850, "is the indifference, indeed the contempt, with which women themselves regard our movement."

Particularly galling was the active hostility of prominent women who had themselves broken out of domestic obscurity, such as Sarah Hale and Catharine Beecher, whose endorsement would have been invaluable. An interesting example of such hostility came from Louisa Cheves McCord of Charleston, South Carolina. The wife of a wealthy banker and journalist, McCord not only ran a large plantation with great efficiency but also contributed to the South's intellectual journals. Boldly and without apology, she took as a proper subject for her pen not women's matters but political economy. She could get away with this because of her social position and be-

cause she was perfectly "sound" on slavery. She missed no opportunity to take a slap both at antislavery agitators and the
women's movement, which she saw as allied in defying the
laws of nature. The Declaration of Independence, she insisted,
was "humbug." *In*equality was nature's law, and the legal and
social subjection of white women to white men, like the slavery of black people, produced a harmonious, familial social
order.

What motivated such women who exemplified the extra-
domestic world that feminists demanded but who remained
strongly opposed to the movement? They usually shared with
feminist leaders class, education, and decisiveness of character.
Among the characteristics that seemed to differentiate the
nineteenth-century women "antis" were a strong commitment
to orthodox, as opposed to liberal, religion, a militant patrio-
tism, and a deep fear of social disorder. Beecher, Hale, and
McCord all saw the subordination of women as part of the
necessary infrastructure of the social order, indeed, as a key
pillar of this overarching social good, and therefore not de-
meaning. Finally, they seem to have had a very strong appre-
hension of male power and of female vulnerability before it.

Feminists assumed that force was becoming much less important in the modern world than in previous eras. Most men
were susceptible of rational persuasion. Once women demonstrated they were in earnest, men would be prepared to share
the world on equal terms with their transformed female col-
leagues. The female antis were far less sanguine. They saw the
superior physical strength of men as a basic given which men
would always be prepared to use against women if provoked.
McCord thought that sheer physical force would always ensure male supremacy. Woman's physical weakness required
protection and, by the law of nature, she was required to buy it
with an abandonment of many natural rights.

To be safe in an inevitably male-dominated world, the antis argued, women needed to adopt a continual conciliatory, non-threatening, and noncompetitive posture toward men. As long as they did so, men would refrain from using their superior strength and would extend their protection and their economic support to women of their own immediate circle. If women abandoned that deferential posture, they would become fair game. "The moment woman begins to feel the promptings of ambition, or the thirst for power," declared Catharine Beecher, "her aegis of defence is gone. All the sacred protection of religion, all the generous promptings of chivalry, all the poetry of romantic gallantry, depend upon woman's retaining her place as dependent and defenceless, and making no claims."

As feminists thought about questions of dependence and power, they realized that the citadel of male strength was marriage, for here the dependence of women and the power of men was most starkly displayed. In marrying, women stepped into a realm of separate law where the protections they had hitherto enjoyed no longer applied. The wife gave up not only her right to control her property but the right to control her person. Even after new laws had made a considerable dent in the principles of coverture, feminists continued to quote Blackstone's chilling words: "The very being or legal existence of the woman is suspended during marriage, or at least is incorporated and consolidated into that of the husband." This judgment epitomized the loss of autonomy, the loss of "self" that feminists saw as the fate of women in traditional marriage.

Outside the movement, too, there seems to have been widespread resentment at two central aspects of women's situation as wife. Women resented their economic dependence: having no separate "purse" of their own, having to ask their husbands for every penny they needed. Many women also resented what they felt were the excessive sexual demands of their husbands. This complaint was important in the philosophy of health and sex reformers, and it was becoming a strong undercurrent in the women's movement as well. With Elizabeth Cady Stanton it became an obsession. "When we talk of woman's right," she wrote to Susan Anthony in 1857, "is not the right to her person, to her happiness, to her life, the first on the list?" With the wife as with the slave, the first right to be secured was the right of "self-ownership," or, as Cady Stanton sometimes expressed it, the right of "self-sovereignty."

In confronting the question of marital power, feminists were entering a real thicket. It was one thing to deprive a husband of rights over his wife's property, quite another to question his marital rights over her body. Feminists were trying to evolve a new model of marriage based upon the same principles of liberal democracy as the state, one that would replace the old common law and religious model. They wanted marriage to be a partnership of equals, in which the autonomy of both partners would be respected. This must mean that the wife should no longer be seen as "surrendering" her body to her husband's use. Since every sexual encounter carried the risk of pregnancy, feminists insisted that it was the wife's right to decide when she would consent to have sex. This was not just a practical question; the wife's "right" to her own body was the essential core of the claim for woman as an autonomous individual. As Lucy Stone wrote to Antoinette Brown Blackwell in 1856, shortly after her marriage:

> It is clear to me that the [marriage] question underlies this whole movement and all our little skirmishing for better laws and the right to vote, will yet be swallowed up, in the

real question, viz has woman, as wife, a right to herself? It
is very little to me, to have the right to vote, to own property etc, if I may not keep my body, and its uses, in my absolute right. Not one wife in a thousand can do that now, &
so long as she suffers this bondage, all other rights will not
help her to her true position.

The new model of sexual relations would depend on educating both partners to the new standard—husbands willingly
to forgo a right, wives to demand one. And if husbands were
not willing to adapt to the new marriage ideal? To Cady Stanton, the solution would have to be divorce. Since 1852 she had
been urging the right, indeed the duty, of wives to divorce
drunken and brutal husbands. In the Temperance movement
tales of drunken husbands abusing their wives was standard
fare; for Cady Stanton, physical violence merged with sexual
violence to create the particular horror of the drunkard's wife.
Permitting divorce for cruelty or even habitual drunkenness
was a proposition that more people were beginning to endorse, yet divorce was a subject that still aroused many fears.
Cady Stanton was determined not only to pursue the question
but by 1860 to expand it and make it central to the women's
movement.

Divorce laws varied considerably from state to state. In
New York the only grounds were adultery; but some states,
especially Indiana and Connecticut, were quite permissive.
Divorce was, in fact, a subject of great public discussion in the
1850s. In late 1852 through early 1853 a major debate on the
subject appeared in the pages of the *New York Tribune* between editor Horace Greeley, the senior Henry James, and the
anarchist Stephen Pearl Andrews. James defended more liberal divorce laws in order to rescue abused wives from brutal
husbands; Greeley totally opposed divorce on any grounds ex-

cept adultery. Andrews was part of a small group of sex radicals advocating "free love."

Free-lovers thought that love and marriage should fall entirely within the private sphere of individual freedom and should not be regulated by the state or the law in any way. They received a good deal of press publicity, and their beliefs were portrayed as leading to total promiscuity, the end of monogamy, and the reign of unbridled lust. Since free-lovers tended also to support women's rights, it was not hard to merge the two movements in the public mind. Not surprisingly, more conservative women in the feminist movement became nervous and anxious to dissociate themselves from seeming to attack marriage. A Boston women's rights convention of 1855 found it necessary to state that "the principles of the Woman's Rights movement are not antagonistic to social, civil and sacred institutions."

Lucy Stone also was beginning to have second thoughts as she realized the divisive potential of agitation over the divorce question, and she tried to deflect Cady Stanton from discussing it in public. But Cady Stanton was not to be deflected. In 1860 divorce was again very much in the public eye. A bill to liberalize the law was before the New York legislature, and once more the *New York Tribune* was publishing a debate on the subject, this time pitting Greeley against Robert Dale Owen. For the first time Cady Stanton was able to attend a national women's rights convention. Her much-anticipated speech turned out to be a bombshell when she offered a number of resolutions on divorce, including the assertion that any compact between human beings that failed to produce or promote human happiness lost all authority. Divorce must be possible, and was desirable, she asserted, not only in cases of cruelty or habitual drunkenness but even when the parties had merely grown not to care for each other.

This speech provoked a major division. Antoinette Brown Blackwell fully upheld a wife's right and duty to leave an abusive or drunken husband but insisted, on religious grounds, that marriage was for life. Therefore divorce, which gave the right to remarry, was wrong. Blackwell did, however, acknowledge that marriage and divorce were proper questions for a women's rights convention. Not so Wendell Phillips, who was so disturbed by this matter that he proposed expunging any mention of Cady Stanton's speech and of the accompanying resolutions from the convention's record. Divorce, he suggested, was extraneous to a movement whose only aim was to gain equal legal rights for women. In fact, once the vote was achieved, he assumed the movement would disband.

Cady Stanton was supported by Anthony and Rose, and the convention voted to reject Phillips's motion not to record. But it adjourned without having taken a position on the liberalizing of divorce laws. Phillips clearly had a great deal of support both inside the convention and out. Many women were disturbed by anything that might threaten the family, and particularly that might undermine the security of the dependent wife. As one of Dall's correspondents wrote, if marriage ties were loosened, "men, wicked ones, I mean, will rejoice at this, because women will be much more in their power than at present." Women could only lose by undermining the stability of the family; one-sided as it was from a woman's point of view, "we should be lost without redemption," she insisted, if the family were destroyed.

Charles Conrad has described the 1860 convention as a crucial moment of redefinition. The issue was not so much whether participants were for or against divorce, but what the contours of the movement should be—what was properly a "woman's issue," and what women's emancipation would mean. Could it be achieved by access to the public sphere and

equal opportunities in education and work, or must it penetrate to the heart of marriage and sexual relations? Such questions would emerge even more starkly after the Civil War
when the movement resumed.

5

Endings and Beginnings

We are all bound up together in one great bundle of
humanity, and society cannot trample on the weakest and
feeblest of its members without receiving the curse in its own
soul.—Frances Watkins Harper, 1866

THE CIVIL WAR buried for the time being the potentially explosive issue of divorce. It did not obliterate the question of women's rights, but it forced feminist leaders
temporarily to pursue the question in different and more cir-
cumspect ways, and eventually it brought in new recruits.
With the war's end, women's rights leaders realized that the
country was at a crucial historical juncture when fundamental
social and political changes might be possible, including even
a formal national recognition of women's equality. As events
unfolded their hopes were dashed, and in struggling to snatch
some gains for women out of postwar America they were
faced with the bitter fact of their irrelevance to the main concerns of their old allies in the antislavery movement. For the
first time the struggles for emancipation from the disabilities
of race and sex diverged, and people who had supported both
causes before the war now had to make difficult political and
moral choices.

The relation of war to women's movements is a rather ambiguous one. War is a supremely masculine event, and it places the highest premium on the virile virtues. "Woman" is to a great extent irrelevant in this masculine drama. True, the enfranchisement of the women of North America and much of Western Europe was achieved in the immediate aftermath of World War I, but this was due much less to women's patriotic war work than to the fact that by 1914 women's movements had grown to be a real and politically embarrassing force whose demands could no longer be slighted. At the time of the Civil War, however, the women's rights movement had reached no such force or maturity. The war brought no major gains for women, though for a brief period feminist leaders deluded themselves that it might. Indeed, under cover of the war excitement, the legislature of New York took the opportunity to *repeal* those parts of the 1861 Married Women's Property Act giving mothers equal right to custody of their children.

For many women the Civil War meant only hardship. For African-American women who had been held as slaves it also meant freedom. What that freedom would mean in practice, and whether it would differ from the freedom gained by black men, remained to be seen. For Northern women in particular, the war did bring opportunities for new kinds of activity and public service. Women's employment rose steeply, and women began to work in new kinds of jobs, including retail stores and business offices. The federal government had earlier begun to employ women as clerks in the Patent Office, but the war provided new openings. By the end of the conflict probably about twenty thousand women, two thousand of them African-American, had served the Union army as nurses, cooks and laundresses. Many Northern women used the managerial skills they had developed in benevolent associations before the war to organize various kinds of relief, supplying soldiers and hospitals. Most of these activities were carried on under the direction of the Sanitary Commission, a voluntary civilian organization which became an indispensable part of the Union's war mobilization. The commission was headed by men, but most of its rank and file were women.

In later years many of the women who had taken these active roles would look back on the war as the period of their lives when they had lived most intensely. Many had become newly aware of their own capabilities and those of other women, and had been disillusioned by the inefficiency and corruption they had witnessed in the male management of the war. Women such as Mary Livermore, a major organizer for the Sanitary Commission in Illinois, the nursing pioneer Clara Barton, and the novelist Louisa May Alcott emerged from the war as committed feminists.

There was no guarantee, however, that new roles played by women during the war would permanently change attitudes or raise consciousness. Clara Barton told a Boston group at the end of the war that the American woman was at least "fifty years in advance of the normal position which continued peace and existing conditions would have assigned her." Women had demonstrated to men and to themselves that they had "character, and firmness of purpose—that she *was* good for something in an emergency." But most people, men and women, interpreted women's war activities as just that: a rising to an emergency.

To men and women who had been involved in the antislavery movement, the war seemed at last an opportunity to end slavery. Abolitionists under Garrison stepped up antislavery agitation. By early 1863 the measure that became the Thirteenth Amendment, abolishing slavery entirely, was in Congress, but some feared it would not pass. Elizabeth Cady

Stanton and Susan B. Anthony determined to put pressure on Congress by rallying massive public support in favor of the amendment. They called a meeting of "Loyal Women" in New York in May 1863 to discuss women's contribution to the war. It was clear, however, that this was not to be just a patriotic rally. "Woman," Cady Stanton wrote, "is equally interested and responsible with man in the settlement of this final problem of self-government." The purpose of the war should be not just the maintenance of the Union but the revitalization of the Republic, completing the unfinished business of the Revolution by finally granting freedom and equal rights to all. War aims such as these would inevitably open up questions of race and gender for the postwar world.

Cady Stanton was making a determined bid for leadership of the women's movement after the war. She had been a figure of great importance and prestige so far because of her vital role in 1848 and because of her important writings and speeches. But her inability to travel because of her young family had kept her away from the national conventions before 1860, thus she had not enjoyed a vital organizational role. She had been one among a group of leading figures. Now the Stanton-Anthony axis was seizing the initiative to take direction of the movement, an initiative it would retain until the end of the decade.

The outcome of the 1863 meeting was the creation of a National Woman's Loyal League, with Cady Stanton as president and Anthony as secretary. Both Lucy Stone and Angelina Grimké emerged from their quasi-retirements to speak on behalf of the moral purpose of the war. Cady Stanton exhorted women to think beyond benevolent work and to understand "the philosophy of the revolution" that was going on, the "irrepressible conflict between liberty and slavery." Not all the audience were attuned to the goals of the leaders. A series of resolutions demanding complete emancipation of all slaves and insisting on their equal citizenship was passed, but another calling for the practical establishment of the "civil and political rights of all citizens of African descent and all women" ran into trouble.

A delegate from Wisconsin objected that "Woman's Rights as an *ism* has not been received with entire favor by the women of the country." She thought that many women from her region would refuse to participate in League activities if it became associated with women's rights. The resolution narrowly passed, but most of the many supportive letters from women that the League received were essentially patriotic endorsements of the war and calls to stamp out disloyalty in the North. Only a few were pleas that the war would end slavery; even fewer made any claims for women.

The meeting decided to undertake a massive petition campaign in support of the Thirteenth Amendment, a revival of the old abolitionist campaigns. Anthony, on a salary of twelve dollars a week, organized the project through contacts in every Northern state. By early 1864 the League had collected more than 100,000 signatures; eventually the number rose to 400,000—far short of the million that had been the goal. Still, the huge rolls of petitions made an indelible impression when carried into the Senate to be presented by Charles Sumner, and in April 1864 the Thirteenth Amendment was passed, abolishing slavery forever.

As soon as the war was over, the Woman's Loyal League disbanded. Feminist leaders determined to resume the women's movement undisguised, where they had left off, by calling the eleventh National Women's Rights Convention. It convened in New York in May 1866, its attendees aware that the times offered a tremendous potential for fundamental change. Two major questions faced the nation: how and on

what terms were the defeated Southern states to be reincorpo-
rated into the Union; and how and on what terms were the
newly freed African Americans to be incorporated into American society. To the women leaders the key question was:
could women take advantage of this opportunity and link
their claims to equality with those of African-American men?

By the time the eleventh national convention met, however,
it was becoming clear that expanding rights for women was of
no concern to the dominant Republican party and of only peripheral importance even to the feminists' old allies in the
antislavery movement. Immediately at war's end, Wendell
Phillips, whose penchant for defining questions very narrowly
had already been illustrated in his opposition to discussing divorce, put the women on notice that "this was the Negro's
hour." Women's claims, he advised, would have to be postponed until the status of black men was settled.

In the summer of 1865 Cady Stanton, via her old friend
Robert Dale Owen, got hold of drafts of the proposed Fourteenth Amendment to the Constitution. One of the most important of all the constitutional amendments, it made the
freed slaves citizens of the United States and asserted that no
citizen could be deprived of rights without due process of law.
In a roundabout attempt to get state legislatures to enfranchise
the freedmen, the amendment added a second clause providing that any state that debarred an adult *male* citizen from
voting should have its representation in Congress proportionately reduced. This amendment would introduce the word
"male" into the Constitution for the first time, making explicit
what had always been implicit: the linkage between citizenship, voting, and male gender.

Feminists immediately realized the importance of this maneuver. Lucy Stone and Henry Blackwell hurried to Washington to try to change the wording. Cady Stanton and

Anthony hastily got up a petition, with ten thousand signatures, asking Congress to enfranchise women (the first such petition to Congress, as opposed to state legislatures). Cady Stanton was determined to turn the unprecedented opportunities of the Reconstruction Era to women's advantage, and, as she put it, "when the constitutional door is open, avail ourselves of the strong arm and blue uniform of the black soldier to walk in by his side." She hoped that the rather covert approach to black male enfranchisement made in the Fourteenth Amendment could be made part of a grand crusade for universal suffrage.

The crusade was to be launched at the May 1866 National Women's Rights Convention. The convention was very well attended; most of the old leaders—Cady Stanton, Anthony, Mott, Martha Wright, Ernestine Rose, Antoinette Brown Blackwell, Caroline Dall, and Frederick Douglass—were there. Wendell Phillips, who in the 1860 convention had made a rousing speech on behalf of enfranchising women, now made a long, curious speech assuring women that the ballot probably would not do much for them, and that what they needed now was an improvement in their own character and attention to questions of work. He was clearly hoping to divert the women from making a nuisance of themselves by pressing for the ballot. Henry Ward Beecher, on the other hand, attending his first women's rights convention, spoke at length in favor of woman suffrage.

Cady Stanton gave the keynote address. In it she moved toward a number of new arguments that would become more central as the century wore on. In particular she took a decidedly patrician tone, urging the women to think of themselves as guardians and champions for the weaker of their sex, like the forty thousand needlewomen of New York City and the multitude of prostitutes on the streets of the great city. Clearly she had a real concern for the poor, for working-class women, and for those driven to prostitution, but equally clearly she did not think of them as part of the "we" whom she was addressing.

Two interesting newcomers spoke at this convention—Theodore Tilton, the young editor of the radical religious newspaper the *Independent*, and the African-American poet and writer Frances Watkins Harper. Harper had been born free in 1825 and explained that she had spent most of her life battling race prejudice. She had not felt as keenly the problems she shared with white women until, as a young widow, she had found her home sold out from under her and her children in order to pay her husband's debts. The thrust of her address, however, was a stern call to white women to recognize their own prejudice and to broaden their conception of "women's rights." "You white women speak here of rights. I speak of wrongs. I, as a colored woman, have had in this country an education which has made me feel as if I were in the situation of Ishmael, my hand against every man, and every man's hand against me."

She went on to recount a number of recent incidents in which she had been prevented from riding in the "Ladies" car on the railroad between Washington and Baltimore, and in which she had been put off streetcars in Philadelphia. Even the renowned Harriet Tubman had been brutally ejected from a streetcar. Tubman had fought, and so had Harper, but "I don't want to have to fight all the time." She demanded of her largely white audience: "Have women nothing to do with this? Are there not wrongs to be righted?" While she did not believe that "giving the ballot is immediately going to cure all the ills of life," still she was for it, for its educational value for whites in particular, if nothing else. The ballot, she said, "is a normal school, and the white women of this country need it. . . . I tell you that if there is any class of people who need to be lifted out of their airy nothings and selfishness, it is the white women of America."

Harper's accounts of the incidents on public transport had been punctuated by cries of "Shame!" and she ended the speech to applause. Susan B. Anthony then moved that the convention resolve itself into the American Equal Rights Association, with the "grand, distinctive, national idea—Universal suffrage," burying "the woman in the citizen," and "women's rights" in "Human Rights." We wish, she explained, "to broaden our Woman's rights platform, and make it in *name*—what it ever has been in *spirit*—a Human Rights platform. . . . As women we can no longer *seem* to claim for ourselves what we do not for others—nor can we work in two separate movements to get the ballot for the disfranchised classes—the negro and woman."

This was a bold move: to clamp the question of women's political status onto that of the freedmen, to broaden the political question of the future of black citizens into a formulation that would force consideration of women and create real universal suffrage at one stroke. One result of this strategy was a greater focus on the ballot. As securing the enfranchisement of black men became a major goal of Republican politicians and reformers, the women's movement was swept along on the same trajectory. Harriet Robinson, a participant and chronicler of the movement, noted that about the time of this convention "the word 'Rights,' as applied to the Woman Movement was changed to that of 'Suffrage.' Mrs. Stanton and others had used the word in convention, but not until 1866–69 did it become the distinctive title of the reform. Since that date, very little has been said about Woman's Rights—but a great deal about Woman Suffrage."

Anthony's resolution was unanimously adopted; Lucretia

Mott was elected president of the new association, with Cady Stanton as the effective vice-president and Anthony as secretary. The session closed with a speech from the venerable Lucretia Mott, who was now in her seventies—a kind of valedictory in which she welcomed a new generation of workers. It was "the proper order of things," she acknowledged, "that the mothers should depart and give place to the children." She singled out "the Tiltons and the Harpers" as "the younger ones" coming forward "to fill our places."

In retrospect this was a poignant choice. Theodore Tilton was removed from the cause within a few years because of his involvement in a spectacular sex scandal. Frances Harper retained an affiliation with the organized suffrage movement, but she never became a central figure in it because the kind of movement she called for, one devoted to "equal human rights," one that would have seen the case of a black woman ejected from a streetcar as very much a women's rights question, never materialized. The American Equal Rights Association lasted until 1870, but it was almost immediately riven by what appeared to be a choice between the rights of black men and the rights of women.

Both the Republican party and antislavery activists increasingly believed that steps must be taken to ensure black male enfranchisement, especially with reports daily by late 1866 of white atrocities against African Americans in the South, and major antiblack riots in Memphis and New Orleans. Once Union troops were withdrawn from the defeated Southern states, only political power would enable the ex-slaves to defend themselves. And once the Southern states were fully restored to the Union, Republicans could maintain a political presence there only through a black electorate. Party politicians and dedicated reformers thus formed a formidable coalition in favor of the enfranchisement of African-American men, making its accomplishment a real possibility—though not a sure thing. None of them wished to complicate matters with the Woman Question.

The women now faced a problem that most movements meet sooner or later: what happens to coalitions when interests that had seemed congruent begin to diverge? Cady Stanton and Anthony made clear their opposition to the Fourteenth Amendment as drafted. At the 1867 convention of the Equal Rights Association, Cady Stanton was asked point-blank whether she opposed enfranchising black men if women did not get the vote at the same time. She replied firmly that she did. "I would not trust him [the ex-slave] with all my rights; degraded, oppressed himself, he would be more despotic with the governing power than even our Saxon rulers are. I desire that we go into the kingdom together, for individual and national safety demand that not another man be enfranchised without the woman by his side."

Having failed to change the wording of the Fourteenth Amendment, feminist leaders turned their attention to prospects in the various states. Major campaigns were mounted in New York, where there was to be a convention to revise the state constitution, and in Kansas, where the question of equal rights was to be put to the people in a very direct way: two separate referenda were scheduled, one on whether the vote should be extended to black men, the other on whether women should be allowed to vote.

Cady Stanton, deciding there was no explicit constitutional prohibition against women holding office, nominated herself for Congress from New York in the 1866 elections and polled twenty-four votes. She also appeared before the suffrage committee of the New York constitutional convention which was chaired by Horace Greeley, now in politics and with presidential ambitions. He put a standard objection to Cady Stanton:

the rights of citizenship came accompanied with obligations; men could vote because they were called upon to fight for their country. Cady Stanton, always quick on her feet, retorted that Greeley himself had not fought in the war; like many other middle-class men, he had paid a substitute. She followed this by reading out the lead names on the petitions she carried; one of them, she read with relish, was Mrs. Horace Greeley. This was a tactical coup but a strategic mistake. Greeley had been a mild supporter of women's rights in the past, but he was now cooling, and this incident deeply offended him. His committee recommended universal manhood suffrage only. This would have been the case anyway; perhaps more important, the movement lost the support of the *Tribune*. Greeley made sure the paper referred to Cady Stanton as little as possible, and always thereafter as "Mrs. Henry Stanton."

In Kansas the outcome was even more disappointing. Here the people were voting directly on the question of universal suffrage, and a number of the most important women's rights leaders put a major effort into the campaign for a "yes" vote on women. In the spring of 1867 Lucy Stone and Henry Blackwell toured the state, speaking extensively for three months; a newcomer on the circuit, the young Olympia Brown, now an ordained minister, replaced them in the summer and fall; Cady Stanton and Susan Anthony came in September and remained through to the election. Stone and Blackwell partly financed their campaign with $1,500 from the Jackson fund for women's rights, over the objections of Wendell Phillips, but money was very tight.

By the time Cady Stanton and Anthony arrived in Kansas in September, it was clear that Republican politicians in the state would be of no help; some, including African-American C. H. Langston, who was convinced that the woman suffrage referendum was a plot to defeat black male suffrage, spoke strongly against women voting. The old antislavery press was strangely silent on the enfranchisement of women. The abolitionist-Republican alliance had decided that the women were a liability, and were cutting them adrift. As a frustrated Cady Stanton and Anthony became increasingly desperate, they made one of the great blunders of their political careers. They joined forces with Democrat George Francis Train, an eccentric railroad promoter and financier, who was making an independent campaign for the presidency. Train was also well known as having been a Southern sympathizer during the war and a rabid racist. But he was quite sincerely in favor of woman suffrage.

According to Anthony's most recent biographer, it was Henry Blackwell who brought Train together with the two women. Blackwell was assuming a dominating role in the women's rights movement and clearly thought of himself as a political mastermind. He had already demonstrated rather blunt moral sensibilities on the question of race, in January 1867 publishing a pamphlet, "What the South Can Do," suggesting a strategy for Southern whites. If the Southern states would institute real universal suffrage, "your five millions of southern white women will counterbalance your four millions of negro men and women, and thus the political supremacy of your white race will remain unchanged."

Blackwell's opportunistic strategy in the Train gambit apparently was that Train would supply much-needed money and bring in Democratic votes; Cady Stanton and Anthony would be able to tone down and contain his racism. It did not work out that way. Train brought in few Democratic votes, but the women's alliance with him offended a great many Republicans. Cady Stanton and Anthony were not able to tone down his racism; instead a good deal of it rubbed off on them, and they began to argue that it was outrageous that ignorant and "degraded" ex-slaves should be enfranchised before educated white women.

Both Kansas referenda were decisively defeated. Cady Stanton and Anthony were disillusioned and bitter over the lack of support from the Republican party in Kansas and the silence of the old abolitionists. "I cannot forgive nor forget the listless do-nothingness of the men we had always believed our best friends," Anthony wrote to Olympia Brown. At the same time many old abolitionists and feminists were finding it hard to forgive Cady Stanton and Anthony for their alliance with Train. In spite of Blackwell's role, Lucy Stone wrote to Olympia Brown that she was "utterly disgusted and vexed." Train's reputation was such that "no decent woman should be in his society." She felt that the women's cause was being "dragged in the dust." But Cady Stanton and Anthony were unrepentant. They had been so certain that in the peculiar circumstances of the postwar reconstruction, suffrage for women was within their grasp that failure in Kansas and what they saw as abandonment by their old abolitionist allies disoriented them. They could no longer count on the antislavery press to report their activities extensively or reprint their speeches in full, and there were no longer specifically feminist journals through which they could spread their views. Train had offered them an unexpected bonanza: a pledge to finance a new weekly newspaper under their direction as a vehicle for women's rights, coupled with his own ideas on politics and money reform. They accepted eagerly. They were prepared to accept "aid from the devil himself," in Anthony's words, if it would advance the cause of women.

The first issue of the new paper appeared in January 1868, with Susan B. Anthony as its proprietor and business manager. Elizabeth Cady Stanton and Parker Pillsbury, one of the few old abolitionists who was still loyal to the women's cause, were the editors. It was given the name the *Revolution*, which raised a number of eyebrows but signaled that it would be a radical, no-holds-barred publication. For the first year a number of pages were devoted to Train's financial hobbyhorses, but he soon left for England, where he was arrested for Irish revolutionary activities. That left the paper entirely under the control of its editors, but it also left it short of money.

The *Revolution* never achieved more than three thousand subscribers, and by 1872 it had collapsed. For four years, however, it was a lively and wide-ranging publication. It contained news of progress on women's rights and on exemplars of women's achievements, and it printed extracts from the writings of Mary Wollstonecraft, Frances Wright, and Auguste Comte. It was an outlet for Cady Stanton's increasingly elitist opposition to the enfranchisement of black men if women were not enfranchised at the same time; but it also printed letters denouncing that view. The paper proclaimed that it would discuss "bread and babies" as well as suffrage, and readers found articles defending the rights of working women and urging them to organize, and articles on infanticide and abortion, divorce, prostitution, the advantages of cooperative housekeeping over the "isolated home," and the "degradation" of loveless marriages. The solution to all these problems, as the *Revolution* saw it, usually was votes for women.

Faced with the indifference or hostility of old allies, Cady Stanton and Anthony began looking about for new ones. They had a few key supporters in Congress, but both party organizations rebuffed them. Both women were drawn to another "outsider group"—labor. After the war Americans suddenly seemed to be living in a new world in which business organizations wielded unprecedented power and a new flamboyant opulence among the rich made disturbingly plain their increasing distance from the growing numbers of the poor. Anthony had always had a special concern for working women; Cady Stanton by mid-1868 had developed a new enthusiasm for the masses as an agent of social regeneration—or, to be more accurate, for the masses as led by women like herself.

The two women first tried to link up with the National Labor Union, an organization of skilled trade unions with broad political goals of labor reform, including land distribution and the eight-hour day. Anthony managed to get herself seated as a delegate at the union's annual congress in 1868, but she was not able to persuade the congress to endorse woman suffrage. In order to provide herself with credentials to attend the congress, Anthony had formed an association of wage-earning women from among the nonunion workers in the print shop where the *Revolution* was produced. It eventually grew to a membership of more than a hundred but lasted barely a year. The working girls' leaders resisted pressure by Cady Stanton and Anthony to call themselves the Working Woman's Suffrage Association, insisting that "the word 'suffrage' would couple the association . . . with short hair and bloomers and other vagaries." They thought that working women should first of all be organized for practical matters concerned with their work; they might get to suffrage later.

The breakup of the association came about partly because its mere existence prompted the male Typographical Union to offer to help the women organize a regular local. Meanwhile, as its original members were drawn more toward regular union organizing, the association was being taken over by middle-class working women, attracted by a group that might address their specific concerns. The new members included a woman doctor, Clemence Lozier, who had been inspired by a Cady Stanton lecture on divorce to get out of a bad marriage and in her mid-thirties train in medicine. Others were a Uni-

versalist minister, Celia Burleigh, and Ellen Demorest, who
had built a highly successful fashion business as the pioneer of
paper dress patterns. To Anthony and Cady Stanton this shift
in membership was appealing, for these were all "working
women," a new type of the independent, self-sustaining, competent woman that had always been their ideal. The association moved its meetings uptown and dues were raised. As the
middle-class women moved in, the earlier working women
moved out, their leader complaining that it was no longer a
real working women's society. Instead of promoting labor interests, it was discussing "irrelevant issues and social problems."

By the end of 1869 the association had crumbled. Cady
Stanton and Anthony's relationship with the organized labor
movement collapsed during a strike called by the Typographical Union, when Anthony suggested to the employers that
they train and employ women. At the next National Labor
Union Congress the delegates voted to expel her. She retali-
ated by asking what efforts they had made to expand their apprenticeship programs to women.

Unlike the women's alliance with the cause of African
Americans, an alliance with organized labor had never been
viable. The women's movement had always defined its main
goal in relation to work as equality of *access*. Trade unions, on
the other hand, were organized on the principle of controlling
the trade, of carefully regulating and restricting access. And
most trade-union men believed that woman's place was in the
home; part of their conception of their own status as respectable skilled men was to be able to support a wife at home,
and they did not see women as part of the permanent working
force. Nor, as the historian Ellen DuBois points out, were
there sufficient numbers of skilled working women who

could have formed a viable feminist constituency and a possible bridge to the labor movement. Most working-class women remained in the kind of low-paid, unstable work that was almost impossible to organize on a long-term basis.

The feminist constituency did change and broaden after the war, as did its leadership, not with the addition of working-class women but from the growing ranks of "new" professional and business women and a number of solidly middle- or upper-middle-class women who had previously held themselves aloof. Three newcomers of the late 1860s were almost instantly catapulted into positions of leadership: Mary Livermore, Isabella Beecher Hooker, and Julia Ward Howe.

Mary Livermore dated her conversion to women's rights to her experience with the Sanitary Commission during the war. She organized an Illinois Woman Suffrage Association in 1868 and in early 1869 started a short-lived suffrage paper, the *Agitator.*

Julia Ward Howe was a rich and aristocratic Bostonian, wife of a well-known reformer, and in addition the famous author of the "Battle Hymn of the Republic." She quickly became the leader of the new New England Woman Suffrage Association, founded in 1868 by a coalition of old feminist-abolitionist men and women who had begun to consider Cady Stanton a liability after her 1860 speech on divorce. They were now deeply offended by her opposition to the Fourteenth Amendment, the alliance with Train, and the radicalism of the *Revolution.* At the founding meeting Howe explained that she had hitherto been put off by what she considered the anti-male rhetoric of the movement, since she had no wish either to attack or to embarrass the men of her family. Now, however, she declared grandly, "the cause had attained such proportions she felt she ought to pay it a tribute of respect." "She ought to do more than to give a mere tribute of respect," muttered Lucy Stone.

Isabella Beecher Hooker was the younger half-sister of Catharine, Henry Ward Beecher, and Harriet Beecher Stowe. Stowe had begun writing articles favoring women's rights in 1865, though she later backtracked. Isabella dated her conversion from reading John Stuart Mill's *The Subjection of Women* in 1869. Having made up her mind, she threw herself into the movement, founding a Connecticut Woman Suffrage Association and by 1871 organizing and largely financing a major national convention.

These three women were roughly the same age as the founding generation of feminists, so they did not represent a younger element. What they represented was a more class-conscious attitude and a deep concern for respectability, refinement, and avoidance of conflict.

Partly as a result of the new women who were joining up, the movement after the war took on a much more solidly prosperous upper-middle-class appearance. When the *New York Tribune* in 1869 slyly asked, "What is to be the costume of the Emancipated Woman?" the sarcastic answer was that "There is evidently an increasing gorgeousness of array upon the platform, wherever she sets her courageous foot." Speakers were visions in black velvet, heavy silk, gold ornaments, and blue satin, and "Mrs. H. B. Stanton . . . discoursed upon the vanities of dress, while arrayed in a brilliant Roman scarf tied over her left shoulder."

Cady Stanton herself was somewhat uneasy, as she admitted in the *Revolution,* with "many of the new converts who, being persons of wealth, refinement, and cultivation, desire to make the platform highly respectable, fashionable, unobjectionable in all ways." She regretted to "hear so much said just now about the importance of keeping our platform clear of all

humble, plainspoken, uncultivated people." Sojourner Truth
was not in the least intimidated by this array of wealth and refinement, and caustically rebuked the women on the platform
at a Rhode Island suffrage meeting. "When I saw them
women on the stage at the Woman's Suffrage Convention, the
other day, I thought, What kind of reformer be you...
dressed in such ridiculous fashion, talking about reform and
women's rights?"

A shift occurred too in the arguments used to support
women's claims to participate in government. Pronounce-
ments on women's moral superiority to men, a minor note before the war, now became more persistent. Feminists began to
speak more often and with particular reverence of motherhood, claiming it gave women a special ethical development
far above that of men, and would enable women to inject a
much-needed moral element into the nation's affairs. This
note was heard most frequently among the "new women." Isabella Hooker, for example, felt that mothers, in their capacity
to create life, approximated God, and that the moral progress
of the nineteenth century would soon recognize that fact by
bestowing increasing honor and power on women. This new
emphasis may have been partly due to the age reached by most
of the women now prominent in the movement—early to
mid-fifties. The power and glory of motherhood is not usually
much celebrated by young mothers actually engaged with
small children. It seems to strike women who are, or who are
of an age to be, grandmothers.

Even Cady Stanton now moved in this ideological direction. By the late 1860s she had read John Stuart Mill, Johann
Bachofen, and Auguste Comte and from these mutually incompatible philosophers took what attracted her. In Mill's
Subjection of Women it was mainly his critique of marriage;
several of his ideas and phrases were absorbed into her own

formulations. Bachofen provided the attractive theory that in prehistory there had been a peaceful matriarchal age in which the foundations of agriculture and civilization had been laid. Cady Stanton took from Comte his exaltation of woman as representing the element of love, which in the coming final stage of human history would reconcile all the antagonistic elements of the modern world into a new harmonious social order based on the religion of humanity. Comte himself had expected women to exert this influence from the safe retirement of the domestic sphere. Cady Stanton ignored this inconvenient aspect of his philosophy and linked women's "essential" and different nature to the possession of political power.

The Fourteenth Amendment was ratified in mid-1868, but the Republicans, concerned that it would not be sufficient to ensure black male enfranchisement, introduced a Fifteenth Amendment stating plainly that states could not withhold the franchise on grounds of race, color, or "previous condition of servitude," thus in effect guaranteeing the vote to black men in all states. Cady Stanton and Anthony immediately proposed that the American Equal Rights Association agitate for the inclusion of the word "sex" among the prohibited grounds. Thus with one simple federal amendment women along with black men would be enfranchised throughout the nation, avoiding all the weary state by state petitioning that had been the only means of proceeding so far. They saw the prospect of a swift and total victory.

As an alternative they began to explore the possibility of a Sixteenth Amendment, to be passed at the same time or soon after the Fifteenth, that would enfranchise women. "This fundamental principle of our government," said Cady Stanton in January 1869, "the equality of all the citizens of the republic— should be incorporated in the Federal Constitution, there to remain forever." Such an amendment was introduced in the House in March 1869 by George Julian of Indiana. It was worded rather differently from what eventually became the Nineteenth Amendment, stating that "the right of suffrage" should be regulated by the *federal* government. In any case, it was neither discussed nor voted on.

The introduction of the Fifteenth Amendment intensified the growing hostility between Cady Stanton and her allies and the old abolitionist/Republican group, including Frederick Douglass, who urged the Equal Rights Association to campaign for its ratification. But Cady Stanton was more than ever determined that black men should not be enfranchised before women. The *Revolution* denounced the Fifteenth Amendment as incomplete and urged that it not be ratified.

To the dismay of many, the language used by Cady Stanton and Anthony in public speeches and in the columns of the *Revolution* was becoming increasingly offensive as their frustration and outrage mounted. "Think of Patrick and Sambo and Hans and Yung Tung who do not know the difference between a Monarchy and a Republic ... making laws for ... Lucretia Mott." The *Revolution* hinted that "outrages" by black men against white women in the South might be expected. The inflammatory nature of such remarks was mitigated by the reflection that the white victim in such cases could not expect much justice from a black male jury who could not help but remember "the generations of wrong and injustice their daughters have suffered at the white man's hands."

Douglass rebuked Cady Stanton in the Equal Rights Association conventions for her reckless use of such epithets as "Sambo." Many years before, in explaining her own objections to being called Mrs. Henry Stanton, Cady Stanton had pointed out that there is much in a name. "Who ever heard a white man called Sambo? . . . . Our colored friends in this country who have education and family ties, who begin to feel the dignity of moral beings, . . . feel insulted if addressed by those familiar names by which their more degraded brethren are known." Now she had forgotten her own insight and her early recognition that all people smart at insult and indignity.

Cady Stanton was not a racist, but she was an elitist. She believed in a kind of Jeffersonian democracy which would be led by an elite not of birth or wealth but of talent and intelligence. Since she was never troubled by false modesty, she saw herself among such an elite, but she would have placed people such as Douglass and Robert Purvis there too. When she objected to "the lower orders" of men being able to legislate for educated and refined women like herself and Lucretia Mott, she lumped together the newly freed slaves, the Irish, and the Germans, the two main immigrant groups of the period. What these groups had in common was not "race" but the fact that in Cady Stanton's eyes they were all peasants: ignorant, unenlightened, and often illiterate. If we accept humiliation as a prime impetus for feminism, then Cady Stanton was humiliated that her gardener or coachmen could now vote while she could not. If truly universal male suffrage was enacted, this would leave sex alone as the brand of exclusion from political participation. In the columns of the *Revolution* she began to advocate an "educated suffrage," that is, that the only qualification for voting should be some kind of literacy test. Literacy, she insisted, unlike sex and race, was a legitimate barrier, even in a democracy, because it was surmountable.

The growing tension between the Stanton-Anthony axis and the majority of abolitionists and many feminists came to a head in an acrimonious debate in the 1869 Equal Rights Association convention. Abolitionist Stephen Foster denounced

Cady Stanton for her racist remarks and tried to oust her from office, and accused Anthony of mismanaging funds into the bargain. Anthony insisted that if a choice had to be made between votes for black men and votes for white women, she was for enfranchising "the most intelligent first. If intelligence, justice, and morality are to have precedence in the government, let the question of woman be brought up first and that of the negro last." Douglass made the unanswerable argument that while the abstract claim to the right to vote was the same for black men and for women, in terms of *need* their situations were very different. "When women, because they are women, are hunted down through the cities of New York and New Orleans; when they are dragged from their houses and hung upon lampposts . . . when they are objects of insult and outrage at every turn . . . then they will have an urgency to obtain the ballot equal to our own."

Someone called out from the audience, "Isn't that true for black women?" Douglass replied: "Yes, yes, yes; it is true of the black woman, but not because she is a woman, but because she is black." The exchange pointed up the person who was being lost in what had become a contest between black men and white women—the African-American woman, who had been the most oppressed under slavery and who, many feminists thought, was not likely to fare much better under a tyrannical husband newly empowered by the marriage laws of free society. Cady Stanton's concern may not have been very deep, but her question was nonetheless well taken when she had asked Wendell Phillips in 1865: "Do you believe the African race is composed entirely of males?" When Phillips and Douglass claimed this was "the Negro's hour," "the Negro" was clearly male. Nor was it as easy as Douglass implied to separate the oppressions of race from the oppressions of sex. When a black woman was gang-raped by marauding

Southern whites aiming at enforcing white supremacy, she was raped because she was a *black woman*.

Lucy Stone had fought for the inclusion of sex in the Fifteenth Amendment for as long as it seemed feasible, but by the May 1869 convention she reluctantly accepted Douglass's arguments and threw her support behind its ratification. Many women who had been involved with both the antislavery movement and the women's rights movement were deeply torn. Paulina Wright Davis and Ernestine Rose supported Cady Stanton. Others sided with the Douglass-Phillips position. Lucretia Mott, Mary Grew, Caroline Dall, Frances Gage, and Abby Kelley decided that their own claims should be postponed until the Fifteenth Amendment was safely ratified. Most African-American participants were in this camp, including Frances Harper, who confessed that "if the nation could only handle one question she would not have the black woman put a single straw in the way, if only the men of the race could obtain what they wanted." "When it was a question of race, she let the lesser question of sex go," and gave a pithy explanation of why: "When I was at Boston there were sixty women who left work because one colored woman went to gain a livelihood in their midst."

The conflict was not intrinsically between race and sex. Phillips insisted that votes for black men and votes for women were "separate questions" and that the government could only handle one at a time. But the women's movement had never considered them to be separate questions; feminists had always insisted that the right to participate in government belonged alike to all adult human beings. Now, for the first time, historical circumstances put black men in competition with women of both races to tap the small amount of available radicalism in American government during this unprecedented window of opportunity. When it became a question of which group should be enfranchised first, the Douglass-Phillips coalition clearly had the better argument. Apart from other considerations, politics is the art of the possible, and the sensible politician throws her weight behind what it is possible to obtain. In the 1860s black male suffrage was radical but just possible; woman suffrage was radical and quite impossible. After a certain point, Lucy Stone accepted this; Stanton and Anthony continued to fight it.

Douglass had the better moral argument too. In assigning priority to the claims of African-American men, he did not need to assert their superiority to women, only that in this particular historical situation the *needs* of the black community were overwhelming. Southern blacks were an identifiable group, subjected to violence and intimidation by whites as a group, with the object of denying them the freedmen's rights they had acquired in the aftermath of war. It was a situation where political power could offer protection. As Frances Harper recognized, African-American women would also benefit from that protection, even if they themselves could not exercise the vote. She was not assenting to permanent inequality for her sex but accepting a strategy that seemed most likely to meet at least some of her needs.

Cady Stanton and Anthony, on the other hand, could offer no such imperative needs-based argument, and so were driven to assert either that educated, refined white women "deserved" the vote more than ignorant, illiterate black men, or that women as a sex had special characteristics that would bring a much-needed new element into government, whereas enfranchising black men would only add more of the same. Their racism was more situational than organic, but that does not excuse it. It was a dangerous departure from their earlier commitment to universal human dignity. Any use of racist language, any labeling of a particular group as inferior helped to naturalize a racist discourse as part of the "normal" vocabulary of debate, even among "progressive" people.

Cady Stanton and Anthony now decided to wash their hands of the Equal Rights Association. At the close of the 1869 convention they hosted a reception for women delegates at the offices of the *Revolution* and there founded a new organization, with Stanton as its president, to be called the National Woman Suffrage Association (NWSA). Its object was to concentrate on the enfranchisement of women, particularly via a Sixteenth Amendment. Lucy Stone and her husband had already left for home; when she heard about the new society she felt deliberately excluded. In November, Stone, Blackwell, Julia Ward Howe, and Thomas Wentworth Higginson called a convention in Cleveland which formed a separate rival organization, the American Woman Suffrage Association (AWSA). It was equally pledged to votes for women, but within a framework that would not interfere with the ratification of the Fifteenth Amendment. Instead it would concentrate its efforts on getting the vote for women through individual state action. AWSA was also determined not to be sidetracked into taking up such "sexual" issues as marriage and divorce.

Early in 1870 a weekly paper, the *Woman's Journal*, was incorporated in Boston, financed by New England suffragists. Stone and Blackwell became the editors and managers, aided by Higginson and Howe. The *Journal* became the unofficial organ of the AWSA and the most important suffrage paper in the country, lasting until 1920 when the vote was finally secured. It was dedicated chiefly to providing news of woman suffrage in the United States and abroad, and often contained long extracts from legislative debates. The *Journal* was clearly intended to be less abrasive and controversial than the *Revolution*. That paper, meanwhile, was in trouble. In May 1870

Stanton and Anthony were forced to hand it over to a woman who had the resources to keep it going, Laura Curtis Bullard, heiress to a patent medicine fortune. Anthony, as the sole "legal proprietor," assumed the entire accumulated debt of the paper, amounting to $10,000. Bullard had written a feminist novel before the war, and the radicalism of the paper scarcely diminished under its new editor, but she could keep it going only for another eighteen months.

One striking difference between the NWSA and the AWSA was the role played by men. Most of the old male feminists allied themselves with the AWSA, and the association made it policy to involve men and appoint them to offices. Its first president was Henry Ward Beecher. The NWSA on the other hand, though it did not exclude men, insisted on having only women officers. Cady Stanton and Anthony felt betrayed by their old male allies and thought they could never rely on men thereafter to make women's issues a priority.

In the first issue of the *Woman's Journal*, in January 1870, Henry Blackwell described the aims of the new AWSA in terms that clearly indicated a narrowing of focus. This wing of the suffrage movement at least would be sharply different from the old prewar movement. The Equal Rights Association, he wrote, had collapsed because "its very name of 'Equal Rights' gave a breadth to the discussions . . . quite incompatible with political efficiency." It had been a body that was "simply a society for promoting justice in human relations, where every question was in order and every speaker entitled to ventilate his opinions. . . . Even the term 'Woman's Rights' covers too wide a field for any possibility of general consent. No two rational human beings fully agree in their definition of these rights." The new AWSA, on the other hand, would be organized efficiently, like a political party, on the base of local societies represented by delegates. And it would have a simple platform—woman suffrage, "on which all can agree without compromising individual opinions on other topics."

Lucy Stone had initially tried to play down the impression that the AWSA was intended as a rival to the NWSA. "I wish I could have had a quiet hour with you, to talk about it," she wrote to Cady Stanton. It was only natural that people should differ as to ends and means, and "the true wisdom is not to ignore, but to provide for the fact." Each association would work for the cause in its own way, so that "your little girls and mine will reap the easy harvest which it costs so much to sow." Her old friends were not mollified and thereafter dismissed "Boston," as they always contemptuously referred to the AWSA, as timid, sectarian, and slaves to narrow propriety.

The division was not necessarily disastrous. The two organizations appealed to and recruited rather different constituencies of women; the lower-key style adopted by the AWSA, and its avoidance of dangerously sexual topics, appealed to numbers of women who would have been offended by the brasher NWSA group. At the same time this allowed the NWSA to be more radical. Lucy Stone explained to one correspondent that the creation of the AWSA provided a home for people who "cannot work with Susan" and were repelled by Cady Stanton's public championing of divorce. The different strategies adopted for getting the vote were complementary, not competing. The antagonism and ill feeling between Cady Stanton and Anthony and Lucy Stone grew rather than diminished over time, but other feminists chose one of the two organizations on the basis of several factors and did not necessarily feel hostile to those in the other group.

Frances Harper allied herself with the AWSA and remained involved in woman suffrage efforts for the rest of her life. In the 1870s Josephine St. Pierre Ruffin, a major black leader, joined the AWSA-affiliated Massachusetts Woman

Suffrage Association. NWSA did not lose all contact with African Americans. Robert Purvis and his wife, and Sojourner Truth remained in its sphere; Harriet Tubman gravitated to the NWSA, as did the journalist Mary Ann Shadd Cary, now a law student at Howard University in Washington, D.C. She attended NWSA meetings in the 1870s and reported on them for the black press. Even the breach with Douglass was repaired, and by 1878 he was again speaking from NWSA platforms.

Both national associations worked to stimulate the organization of state and local woman suffrage associations around the country. Cady Stanton and Anthony had toured the Midwest in early 1869, leaving newly converted suffragists and societies in their wake. Stone traveled extensively throughout New England, organizing subsidiary societies. Even in the South there were stirrings. Woman suffrage societies were formed in Missouri and Virginia. In South Carolina the prominent African-American Rollin sisters led an interracial woman's suffrage organization, and Charlotte Rollin was their delegate to the 1871 AWSA convention in New York. All this organizational activity marked an important new departure for the women's movement. Its leaders were reaching out to new constituencies and attempting to refound the movement on the basis of a network of *organized* women. The conversion of a women's rights movement into woman suffrage organizations, while on the one hand narrowing its scope, can also be viewed as a salutary focus. Movements that do not solidify into organization die.

On the negative side, the organized movement was now decisively split. There would be various desultory attempts to merge the two groups in the next few years, but until 1890 they remained separate. The two most dynamic feminist leaders, Cady Stanton and Anthony, had broken their historic con-

nection with the old abolitionist allies and with it a dedication
to a broad conception of natural human rights. While Stone's
AWSA had not made this break, in effect the determination
of the friends of black male suffrage not to contaminate their
cause with women's rights had forced the feminists who
agreed with them into focusing narrowly on women. Worse,
in reacting to the Fourteenth and Fifteenth Amendments
some feminists had succumbed to the always available racist
strains in American society.

Ellen DuBois, in her pathbreaking *Feminism and Suffrage*,
interprets the events of the late 1860s positively. Taking Cady
Stanton, Anthony, and the NWSA as the mainstream of feminism, she views their separation from the old abolitionist alliance as a "weaning" of the women's movement away from its
role as junior partner to antislavery, enabling it to mature and
develop its own constituency and set its own agenda. More re-
cently, historians have posed more searching questions about
the Stanton-Anthony refusal to support the Fifteenth Amendment and the racist cast of their arguments; and DuBois has
since acknowledged that she did not pay sufficient attention to
the issue of racism.

The opposition of Cady Stanton and Anthony had no effect
on the passage of the Fifteenth Amendment, which was ratified in 1870, but it did cut them off from old friends and from
the generous human rights philosophy of their own past. The
NWSA by no means concentrated solely on the franchise in its
early years, but as an organization it did not consider racial
discrimination to be part of the "degradation" it chose to combat. Cady Stanton and Anthony, as individuals, sometimes deplored white Southern efforts to undo Reconstruction. Lucy
Stone, in the *Woman's Journal*, denounced the spread of segre-
gation laws in the South, but the AWSA as an organization
did not emphasize the connection between racism and sexism.

Feminists no longer looked upon struggles over racial oppression as central to the continuing universal contest between tyranny and freedom, of which they had once thought the woman's movement to be a part. Even had a united woman's movement remained committed to a vision of human rights as rooted in "needs" and "wants," it would have lacked the political strength to counter the rollback of Reconstruction. It might, however, have been able to stave off the racism to which it succumbed itself in the 1890s.

6

Sex and Suffrage

We progress in our social theories in part by the growth of ideas in our minds, in part by the growth of ideas in the social medium which surrounds us, and in part by the growth in us of that boldness which dares say openly what we do think.— Elizabeth Cady Stanton (1870)

PRIORITIES OF RACE and gender had split the women's movement; issues of sexuality threatened to derail it altogether. In the early 1870s the involvement of the NWSA with a notorious free-love exponent, Victoria Woodhull, the peripheral involvement of Cady Stanton and Anthony with several sensational trials with a sexual theme, and finally the fact that two prominent male feminists were the protagonists in one of the most publicized sex scandals of the century, all provided plenty of ammunition for opponents of the movement and frightened off a good many women.

Accusations of free love that had sometimes been flung at the movement before the war resurfaced in the late 1860s. They were sufficiently intimidating to some newcomers that Mary Livermore, at the 1869 Equal Rights Association meeting, introduced a resolution affirming that while the movement wished to remove the legal disabilities of women in marriage, "we abhorrently repudiate Free Loveism as horrible and mischievous to society, and disown any sympathy with it." The West, she insisted, demanded some such reassurance. So did New England, according to Phebe Hanaford, a Universalist minister, who said "she had heard people say that when women endorsed woman suffrage they endorsed Free Loveism." Old-timers Stone, Anthony, and Ernestine Rose managed to squelch the resolution, pointing out that explicitly to deny something so patently untrue was to concede too much to the enemy. But the issue would not go away, partly due to the actions of Elizabeth Cady Stanton.

Cady Stanton, though she insisted on the importance of the ballot, remained convinced that marriage was at the heart of women's oppression. The *Revolution* still echoed her ideas even under its new editor. "The woman question is more than a demand for suffrage," it declared. Its "true foundations do not rest on the surface of her citizenship, but in the heart of her womanhood.... The solemn and profound question of marriage ... is of more vital consequence to woman's welfare, reaches down to a deeper depth in woman's heart, and more thoroughly constitutes the core of the woman's movement, than any such superficial and fragmentary question as woman's suffrage."

Cady Stanton not only used the *Revolution* as a vehicle for her views on easier divorce but spoke out boldly on the subject. The divorce rate in America had in fact risen considerably after the war, prompting moralistic condemnation from press and pulpit, and the beginnings of a move to significantly tighten divorce laws. To Cady Stanton, however, more divorces were not a cause for alarm but a sign that women were beginning to break their chains. "It is sheer folly at this age of the world," she told the May 1870 NWSA convention, "to waste ink or words on marriage as an indissoluble tie and on the husband's divinely ordained authority." She affirmed that she did wish to revolutionize marriage and the family as her critics charged; she wished to transform an authoritarian institution into a republic, to make the intimate private realm conform to the democratic practice of the public. Marriages contracted by mature people, both of whom were able to support themselves, and which could be ended when the marriage ceased to be happy, would, she insisted, elevate marriage to a much higher plane of friendship and mutual cooperation. As she told a small private gathering, freedom was the ultimate human value and must include "freedom to repair mistakes."

The fact that most divorce cases were initiated by women indicated that many women did find liberal divorce laws a welcome avenue of escape. Others, even in the women's rights camp, thought the divorce laws should instead be tightened. Isabella Beecher Hooker, for example, after the split had allied herself with Cady Stanton, but she campaigned in Connecticut to make that state's rather permissive divorce laws more restrictive. She claimed that among the woman suffrage supporters she knew, "there are probably fifty who would favor a restriction of our divorce laws where there is one who would keep them as they are." Lucy Stone had always favored divorce as a remedy for drunkenness or gross cruelty, but she was increasingly disturbed at the idea of easy divorce. As she wrote in the *Woman's Journal* in 1874, easy divorce might well mean in practice the "freedom of unworthy men to leave their wives and children to starve, while it could not give similar freedom to mothers to leave their children."

Thus Cady Stanton's determination to make liberalized divorce a women's issue deepened the aversion that many women felt toward the NWSA wing of the movement. Lucy

Stone and the AWSA leadership were becoming increasingly anxious to dissociate themselves from Stanton's radical statements. "As friends of Women Suffrage," wrote Henry Blackwell sternly, in the *Woman's Journal* in June 1870, "we protest against being compromised in this matter by the ultraism of a few individuals." Five months later the *Journal* warned its readers frankly: "Be not deceived—*free love means free lust.* And let all women ponder well how they accept the specious arguments, and follow the leading of even a woman beloved and honored as Mrs. Stanton is, and has been, if her teaching lead in that direction."

Yet it was clear that issues involving sexuality stirred the interest and indignation of many women in ways that calls for suffrage did not. In 1869, for example, the Pennsylvania case of Hester Vaughan, a twenty-year-old immigrant domestic servant who had been seduced by her employer and who was sentenced to be hanged for infanticide, evoked a vast outpouring of female sympathy. The *Revolution* immediately took up the case, pointing out that Vaughan had of course been tried by an entirely male court and jury. Cady Stanton and Anthony lobbied the governor and called a public protest meeting that attracted more than a thousand women. Vaughan was pardoned, and Cady Stanton and Anthony collected money to enable her to return to England.

Even more sensational was the McFarland-Richardson case of 1870, in which an abusive husband, Daniel McFarland, shot the lover of his ex-wife, who had just secured a divorce for cruelty. The lover, Albert Richardson, was a reporter for the *New York Tribune.* Before he died he was married to the former Mrs. McFarland, by no less than Henry Ward Beecher, in the presence of Horace Greeley. After a highly publicized trial, McFarland was acquitted on grounds of temporary insanity and then granted custody of his young son. Cady Stanton and Anthony used public interest in the trial to call attention to the unequal situation of men and women in marriage. They called a women-only public meeting to discuss the affair, and two thousand turned up. To Cady Stanton, the whole business was a perfect demonstration of the male belief that a man "owned" his wife, even to the extent of killing her lover, and even after she was no longer legally his wife. Defense counsel had in fact alluded to the biblical supremacy of the husband over the wife and his right to defend his property in her.

Feminists such as Stone, Livermore, and Julia Ward Howe held themselves aloof from such occasions, and feared the dangerous sexualization of the women's cause that Cady Stanton seemed to be pursuing. Advocacy in such cases could indeed backfire, as Anthony found in 1871 when she and Cady Stanton were on a joint lecture tour in California. They publicly defended a prostitute, Laura Fair, who had shot her lover, a prominent attorney, when he refused to keep his promise to leave his family and marry her. Fair was sentenced to death; Cady Stanton and Anthony visited her and, as in the two earlier cases, called a public meeting of protest. Both women made the unfaithful husband the villain, who had deceived and used both his wife and his mistress; but this time public opinion was far more hostile to the accused woman. Anthony in particular bore the brunt of public and press displeasure. In all three of these cases, Anthony and Cady Stanton had tried to harness public interest and sympathy for "wronged" and abused women to an acceptance of a feminist analysis of why such cases could occur. But the public willingness to accept such analysis was narrowly limited.

Cady Stanton and Anthony each spent a good part of the 1870s on the lecture circuit now that they were no longer tied down by the *Revolution*. The development of a railroad network and the completion of a transcontinental line made it easier for Eastern-based feminists to travel widely, spreading suffrage ideas and where possible organizing. Anthony used her lecturing to pay off the *Revolution* debt, which she managed in six years. Cady Stanton signed up with the Lyceum circuit, maintained a grueling pace, but earned a good deal of money. She had a number of lectures in her repertoire; the most popular were "Our Girls," a rousing call to educate young women to vigorous independence, and "Home Life," whose reassuring title actually masked a defense of liberalized divorce. By her mid-fifties she had become quite fat, but she was still energetic and had the knack of being able to catnap at any opportunity. Motherly, good-humored, and witty, people took to her, so she could get away with radical statements that would bring poor Anthony public denunciation.

Several times throughout her Western tours, Cady Stanton gave a woman-only lecture on "marriage and maternity." This was becoming a standard part of her repertoire, one which she claimed elicited a response from her audience that suffrage never could. Many women brought her personal stories of sexual and physical abuse. Her object, she explained, was to spread the "new gospel of fewer children, and a healthy, happy maternity." There was a good deal of hostile speculation as to what exactly went on in these meetings, with no reporters allowed. The only printed account we have comes from a reporter of the *San Francisco Chronicle*, who apparently attended a lecture disguised as a woman. If his report is accurate, nothing very startling was said.

Cady Stanton gave sensible advice on the care of babies and declared that birth need not be a great trial to a strong and healthy woman. But she also insisted that girls must not be educated to think that their entire purpose in life was motherhood. She repeated what had become an obsession, that much insanity, mental retardation, even crime was due to heredity and that women impregnated by drunken or licentious husbands were likely to produce diseased and "idiot" children. It was women's duty to escape from such marriages, and even in good marriages to reduce the number of children they bore. "It is of more importance what kind of a child we raise than how many," she proclaimed. "It is better to produce one lion than twelve jackasses. We have got jackasses enough."

Her insistence that it was woman's duty *not* to have too many children, and her plea for self-sovereignty and a woman's right to control her own body, probably did inspire and inspirit many women who heard her. "What radical thoughts I then and there put into their heads," she wrote exultantly to Elizabeth Smith Miller; she was sure "these thoughts are permanently lodged there!" But her replies to specific questions from the audience were vague and not very helpful. When one asked how a woman was to remain "sovereign of her own person" when her husband did not agree, Cady Stanton replied airily that men must be "educated up to the higher civilization." When another wondered timidly about contraception, "Mrs. Stanton promptly replied that such views of the matter were too degrading and disgusting to touch upon" and must be classed as a crime, along with infanticide.

By the late 1880s Cady Stanton had changed her mind and at least in private was prepared to endorse the use of contraception, as well as to acknowledge the reality and desirability of sexual passion in women. But in the 1860s and 1870s her views on artificial birth control were in the mainstream of feminist thinking. In this the women's movement was at odds not only with the position of some of their own radical allies such as Robert Dale Owen, who in the 1830s had published birth-control methods, but of the practice of many women.

The accelerating decline in the birth rate throughout the nine-teenth century may have been partly due to agreed abstinence among couples and to widespread abortion, but part of it was also doubtless due to a quiet, unpublicized use of various artificial contraceptives.

As the historian Linda Gordon has pointed out, the attitude of leaders of the women's movement toward issues of contraception is puzzling. Feminists usually recognized that sexual desire was as natural to women as to men, and they certainly endorsed "birth control," in the sense of a purposeful human control over reproduction. The pathetic, worn-out, prematurely aged mother of too large a brood was a stock figure of feminist discourse. Woman's "self-sovereignty," her right to decide when she would become a mother, had become a central tenet of the movement. "Without control of one's person," declared NWSA stalwart Matilda Joslyn Gage at an 1876 convention, "the opportunities of the world, which are the only means of development, cannot be used."

Yet all feminists seemed to recoil from the idea of mechanical contraception; birth spacing was to be achieved through abstinence. While many male moralists objected to contraception on the grounds that removing fear of pregnancy would free women to become promiscuous, feminists seem to have suspected that removing the possibility of unwanted children to support would license men to demand unlimited sex of their wives. For feminists who sought for women the sole control of their own bodies, anything that might place those bodies at the disposition of men could not be tolerated. There also seems to have been a kind of romantic recoil from the calculation involved in the use of contraception. *"To live straight on,"* wrote Caroline Dall, denouncing the use of contraceptives as degrading, "is the only wholesome way to live."

One of the major methods of birth control in the mid-nineteenth century seems to have been abortion, which the *New York Times* in 1871 called "The Evil of the Age." By the 1860s the medical profession, led by the American Medical Association, was mounting a steady campaign against what it portrayed as a rising tide of abortions among vain, self-indulgent middle-class married women trying to avoid their natural duties of motherhood. The few feminists who ever mentioned abortion, such as Cady Stanton, always condemned it. But they interpreted abortion as part of the general victimization of women. They assumed that abortions were sought by women who had been made pregnant out of wedlock, were desperately poor, or were reluctant to bear children with the brutal stamp of drunken husbands upon them. They condemned the act but not the women, implying that better economic opportunities for women, freer divorce, and a right ordering of marriage into a relationship of equality and mutual respect would substantially reduce the recourse to abortion.

The 1870s brought a conservative reaction to what many people saw as the sexual license and moral breakdown of the postwar years. As the number of divorces grew, so did worry that the family was falling apart; there appeared to be a rise in the number of illegitimate births, abandoned children, wife murders, and shootings of husbands or lovers. Sexual scandals and the well-publicized sexual flamboyance of public figures provoked a reaction. From the mid-1870s there was less tolerance of sexual experiment, criticism of marriage, or descriptions of contraception than in the years before the war. In 1873 the so-called Comstock laws gave police and the courts considerable powers of censorship over forms of public expression and forbad the use of the mails for anything the courts might decide to be "obscene." Information on contraception was so classified, and books on the subject were now driven underground. Thus it would have been difficult in any case for the women's movement openly to discuss contraception. But while feminists generally believed that rational discussion of sexuality should not be suppressed, they shared Comstock's estimate of contraception as obscene.

They also shared a growing public preoccupation with prostitution, which feminists had always seen as a prime example of male oppression of women. After the Civil War a new police approach to prostitution appeared, spearheaded by medical men. Alarmed at the rise of venereal disease and assuming that prostitution was a feature of urban life that could never be erased, a number of doctors, police officials, and lawyers proposed to end the vague legal status of prostitution by subjecting the trade to strict regulation, including medical inspection of the women. In effect they would license it. Among feminists, the legalization of prostitution—the official recognition of a certain class of women as designated sex objects for male use—provoked a visceral reaction. The existence of prostitution was to feminists what the existence of slavery had been to free African Americans before the Civil War: a visible, humiliating reminder of the degradation to which people like themselves could be reduced. To the regulationists the question was one of public health; to feminists it was a question of the status of women.

Susan B. Anthony was especially active in fighting state efforts at regulation. She aroused enough press and public indignation in 1871 to defeat a proposed regulation bill in New York. In the 1870s a number of states and cities attempted regulation, but these efforts were almost always foiled by the efforts of coalitions of reformers, including large contingents of organized women. In Boston, Lucy Stone and Mary Livermore, as well as William Lloyd Garrison and Wendell Phillips, became members of a committee to combat regulation. A new crusade for "social purity" arose, separate from the woman suffrage movement but with a good deal of overlap, aiming to eradicate prostitution altogether and bring male sexual practices up to the standard demanded of respectable women. This was a project to which most feminists were extremely sympathetic. Anthony added a lecture on social purity to her repertoire, and it became one of her most popular.

The relation of sexual issues to the women's movement came to a head in the early seventies through the involvement of the notorious Victoria Woodhull. Woodhull was an adventuress who dabbled in spiritualism, socialism, advanced ideas on sex, women's rights, and occasional blackmail. In 1869 she and her younger sister, Tennie C. Clafflin, had been set up on Wall Street by a besotted Commodore Cornelius Vanderbilt as the first women stockbrokers. They attracted much publicity and made a good deal of money. The Woodhull entourage soon came to include Stephen Pearl Andrews, one of the period's most colorful reformers, whose belief in the absolute sovereignty of the individual had been the philosophical basis of his defense of divorce in the prewar newspaper debate with Horace Greeley and Henry James, Sr. Andrews became Woodhull's intellectual mentor; he may have written much of the material published under her name, and many of her speeches, but she also seems to have adopted his ideas as her own.

Woodhull's interests increasingly turned toward American politics and women's rights, and in April 1870 she sent a letter to the *New York Herald* announcing herself as an independent candidate for the presidency of the United States. She and her sister launched a newspaper as part of her campaign: *Woodhull and Clafflin's Weekly*, a lively vehicle for their championship of spiritualism, legalized regulated prostitution, "free love," and divorce, as well as socialism, currency reform, and land reform. The paper supported various labor causes and in December 1871 was the first American periodical to print the Communist Manifesto. It also specialized in exposés of various government and business frauds, of which Gilded Age America supplied an abundance. To this point Woodhull had had little contact with the organized women's movement, but this was soon to change. Within the next five years she almost took control of the NWSA while simultaneously providing the movement with a good deal of highly unfavorable publicity.

In October 1869 a new approach to gaining the vote, quickly dubbed the New Departure, had been suggested by the president of the Missouri Women's Suffrage Association, Virginia Minor. Worked out by her lawyer husband, it was based on the assertion that voting was a natural right of citizenship, enshrined in the Constitution and reaffirmed by the recent Fourteenth Amendment, which guaranteed those rights to "all persons" born or naturalized in the United States. Women were thus citizens and therefore already *had* the right to vote. All they had to do now was exercise it. States that refused to let women vote would be violating both the spirit and the letter of the Constitution. They could then be sued for a violation of civil rights, and the whole issue would be decided in the courts.

Much of this strategy was appealing. It offered a new kind of decisive action; it was a shortcut that would obviate more years of tedious and probably unsuccessful propaganda and petition work; and it was based on an intellectual proposition that the women's movement had always maintained—that voting was a natural right. The *Revolution* published Minor's idea and distributed ten thousand extra copies of the issue, including copies to every member of Congress.

It was Woodhull, however, who induced the NWSA to adopt New Departure philosophy and tactics as official strat-

egy. In late 1870 she sent a memorial to Congress on woman
suffrage, using essentially the Minor argument, with the addition that the wording of the Fifteenth Amendment should not
be taken to permit other reasons for denying the vote, in addition to those explicitly prohibited. In January 1871 she was invited to address the House Judiciary Committee to support
her position. She asked Congress to pass a simple declaratory
act, merely affirming and endorsing the prior right of women
to vote. Her appearance and her speech made a great impression, not only on the congressmen (though not enough to
make the majority accept her position), but also on Susan B.
Anthony and Isabella Beecher Hooker, who were both in the
House to hear her. The women invited Woodhull to address
the NWSA convention that was then meeting in Washington.
She bowled over the convention, as she had others, and in her
wake the NWSA enthusiastically decided to postpone agitation for a Sixteenth Amendment and adopt the New Departure. Anthony set off on a Midwestern lecture tour to
persuade women that they already had the right to suffrage
and that at the next election they should attempt to register to
vote.

Woodhull now became the favorite of important NWSA
leaders. Cady Stanton had not been at the convention and had
not yet met Woodhull, but Paulina Wright Davis and Isabella
Hooker were especially taken with her. To Anthony she was
new blood for the cause: she was young (thirty-three), good-
looking and glamorous, had new and bold ideas, and, not
least, was prepared to pledge $10,000 to the movement.
AWSA leaders in Boston, on the other hand, were skeptical of
Woodhull's somewhat dubious reputation and were not enthusiastic about the New Departure tactic. Elsewhere individual feminists also voiced their disquiet with a maneuver that
seemed like trickery. She did not wish to gain her rights

"through a back door which had been left ajar by accident," declared the leader of the woman suffrage association of Iowa.

Meanwhile the press, led by the *New York Tribune*, was turning up damaging information about Woodhull's unconventional private life, and she herself was becoming ever more open about her sexual views. The fact that Woodhull was now thoroughly allied with the women's movement allowed the press to claim that what they had suspected all along was true: feminism led inexorably to free love! This time the accusations seemed more plausible and stuck more firmly. The NWSA convention in May 1871 affirmed a series of resolutions offered by Paulina Wright Davis, asserting the primacy of social/sexual rights over political rights. Freedom, said Davis, influenced by Woodhull, is one principle and must be reflected in the social as well as the political realm. The most basic of all rights for women was the "right of self-ownership."

"Self-ownership" was turning out to be an ambiguous term. As Davis used it—and few of the women's rights leaders would have disagreed—it meant the right of a wife to withhold sexual relations from her husband. Woodhull often used the phrase in that sense too; on the other hand, she sometimes used it to imply a woman's right to follow her sexual inclinations in whatever way she wished. In November, in a sensational speech in New York, Woodhull defiantly affirmed, "Yes, I am a Free Lover!" and added that it was her *inalienable, constitutional,* and *natural* right to love anyone she chose, for as long or as little as she chose, and to change that love every day if it pleased her. Furthermore, she told her startled audience, "it is your duty to see that I am protected" in that right. To make freedom of sexual expression a constitutionally protected right may have been an anticipation of the twentieth-century discovery of a "right of privacy," but to a mid-nineteenth-century public it meant total sexual license and de-bauchery.

Free love was to the nineteenth-century women's move-ment what lesbianism has been to the twentieth. The linkage of feminism with the specter of deviancy from the sexual norms of society deflected public attention from a serious en-gagement with the aims of the movement, provided an easy derogatory label, and frightened off a good many women. Across the country, woman suffrage associations hastened to issue statements dissociating themselves from Woodhull, dis-avowing any inclination toward free-love doctrines, and in-sisting they believed in the Bible and in marriage, and that woman suffrage would in no way weaken these bastions of the social order. Some purged leading members who seemed even slightly unsound on the issue. "Too many of our friends lack *moral courage*," wrote a male sympathizer to Amelia Bloomer in Iowa, "the first sneering cry of 'Free Love' puts them to flight."

Cady Stanton, who had now also succumbed to Woodhull's charm, continued to defend her from her detractors, but An-thony decided that Woodhull was becoming a distinct liabil-ity. In May 1872 she managed to block a Woodhull move to take over the NWSA and merge it with her own fledgling po-litical party, through which she intended to run for president on a platform that mixed socialism, populism, and "social freedom." Woodhull was by now under constant bombard-ment from a hostile press, and her finances were in bad shape. But she still had a trump card up her sleeve. In November 1872 she published an article in the *Weekly* accusing Henry Ward Beecher, a married man and the most famous preacher in America (as well as a past-president of the American Woman Suffrage Association), of having had a long-standing affair with the wife of his friend, Theodore Tilton, the well-known editor and women's rights activist. Self-righteously, Woodhull declared that she wished only to expose the hypocrisy of men like Beecher, who preached a strict sexual morality and denounced principled free-lovers like herself while they themselves were thoroughly promiscuous. It was not the love affair she objected to, because she believed that men and women should be free to follow their sexual and emotional inclinations; it was Beecher's attempt to cover up and deny what he was doing.

The article was immediately taken up by the nation's press and provoked print and public speculation for the next three years. During this time Beecher was first tried by his church, and acquitted, and then faced a civil trial when Tilton sued him for alienation of his wife's affections. Beecher admitted to overaffectionate manners but denied wrongdoing, and with a jury unable to reach a verdict he was again acquitted. Beecher's career was not seriously damaged by the scandal. Tilton, on the other hand, was ruined by the costs of the case, and left the United States to retire to France. The real loser was his wife, Elizabeth Tilton, who spent the rest of her life alone, embittered, and impoverished. Since all the major players were involved with the women's rights movement, the scandal was yet another piece of evidence that feminism equated to promiscuity.

Woodhull's whistle-blowing broke the spell for most of her suffrage supporters. "I am happy to tell you," Mary Livermore reported to an Illinois colleague, "that the offensive alliance between Mrs. Stanton, Mrs. Hooker and Miss Anthony and Mrs. Woodhull is at an end. They became convinced that she was all that we had told them, finally." Woodhull herself began to backtrack on many of her more forward positions. She split with the spiritualists, insisted she was really concerned with the purity of marriage, divorced her husband,

and in 1877, with her sister, left the United States for England, where both women eventually married wealthy Englishmen and lived out the rest of their long lives in comfort and respectability. Victoria continued to be interested in reform and wrote a good deal on the importance of the eugenic breeding of children. She also tried to rewrite her own story, claiming she had never really been a free-lover and that the more scandalous articles in *Woodhull and Clafflin's Weekly* had been inserted without her knowledge while she was busy elsewhere.

It is difficult to know what finally to make of Victoria Woodhull. Most recent historians take her more seriously than those in the past. That her articles and speeches may have been chiefly written by someone else means only that she anticipated the common practice of modern politicians. There is no reason to suppose they embodied ideas in which she did not firmly believe. She turned out to be an extremely effective speaker and publicist, and was clearly a charismatic and engaging personality. Her modern defenders point out that the constitutional arguments she contributed to the women's cause, as well as some of the economic reforms she championed, were serious and worth attention. What undermines her credibility most is less her erratic behavior in the 1870s than her disavowal in the 1880s of her radical past.

Her impact on the women's movement was on the whole disastrous. While she gingered up the NWSA briefly in 1871, the major effect of her involvement was to strengthen the movement's enemies. In a number of state campaigns of the 1870s to include woman suffrage clauses in new constitutions, the issue of free love was continually flung at the suffrage workers. In Iowa in 1872, Republican leaders decided not to put a woman suffrage amendment to a popular vote in view of the current storm of accusations and innuendos about free love. "This Beecher-Tilton affair is playing the deuce with WS in Michigan," wrote the campaigning Henry Blackwell to Lucy Stone back in Boston. "No chance for success this year I fancy!" The free-love charges also tended to drive many feminists into greater timidity and narrowness. After Woodhull it was harder for the movement openly to explore issues involving sexuality, except in strictly moralistic terms, as in the social purity movement against prostitution.

The furor over free love and the whole Woodhull debacle only confirmed AWSA leaders in their belief that a clear focus on the ballot was the only way to keep the movement from disintegrating. Women involved with the AWSA had an instinctive revulsion from the "sexual" route apparently taken by the NWSA, and the men who participated and wrote for the *Women's Journal* were clearly much more comfortable with a clear-cut, constitutionally argued, narrow demand for the vote than with the rhetoric of liberation that had been the hallmark of the prewar movement and that Cady Stanton still tried to maintain.

Looking back on the 1850–1851 conventions, wrote Thomas Wentworth Higginson condescendingly in the *Journal* in 1870, "the claim for suffrage is buried under such a load of words that you can hardly find it, while they ascend very far into dim air in their other demands.... This rather vague and high-flown element in the movement was fortunately met and controlled by an element of clear common sense." "The Boston managers of the American Woman Suffrage Association have abandoned nine-tenths of the woman question, and are devoting themselves only to the other one-tenth," countered the *Revolution*, insisting that Stone, Higginson and Co. were far more conservative than the 1848 originators of the movement.

But the position taken by the AWSA leaders had much to

be said for it. Claiming the vote was certainly radical, as witness the strength and determination of the opposition to woman suffrage, but it was a radicalism that pitted a united movement against the outside world. Sexual issues, on the other hand, divided the movement itself. It could be argued that suffrage, as the preeminent symbol of woman stepping out of her confined domestic sphere, of woman as human being and citizen rather than a creature defined mainly by her sex, epitomized the central theme of the prewar women's rights movement.

By 1870 some small successes had been registered on the suffrage front. After the humiliating defeat in Kansas came one ray of hope from the West. In December 1869 the territorial legislature of Wyoming extended the suffrage to women, and early the next year women in the territory of Utah were also given the vote. In themselves these events did not mean much. Territorial voters could not vote in presidential or congressional elections but only for the territorial legislature. And suffrage had been won for reasons that had little to do with equality for women or the activities of women's rights advocates. Democrats in the Wyoming legislature wished to advertise the territory and embarrass the Republican governor at the same time. The Mormon establishment in Utah sought to deflect Eastern criticism of polygamy by demonstrating that Mormon women were not downtrodden.

The West was not in fact a particularly fertile field for a women's movement. Generally speaking, women's rights organizations usually sprang up because Eastern activists had either moved West or toured the region. They often languished once the stimulus was removed. An exception was San Francisco, where the first suffrage paper in the West, the *Pioneer*, was begun in 1869 by a twenty-five-year-old teacher, Emily A. Pitts. A native of New York, she does not appear to have been a feminist activist until she came to California. One of the contributors to the *Pioneer* during its short life was Abigail Scott Duniway of Portland, Oregon. The mother of six children, with an invalid husband, in 1871 she started a much longer-lived suffrage paper, the *New Northwest*, and lectured extensively for the woman's movement. Her paper kept the cause alive on the West Coast, but no strong organization emerged.

While press and public focused on free love, the New Departure strategy moved ahead. In 1871 in Washington, D.C., Mary Shadd Cary succeeded in registering to vote, and addressed the House Judiciary Committee on her rights to suffrage as a taxpayer. Other Washington women, who had been denied registration, sued the election officials and lost. In the presidential election of 1872 at least 150 women, and probably more, tried to vote, including Sojourner Truth, Virginia Minor, and Susan B. Anthony.

Anthony and a group of fifteen other women persuaded the election inspectors to accept their votes, Anthony promising the men that if there were legal consequences she would cover their legal costs. Three weeks later she was arrested for the crime of having voted unlawfully. This was an unexpected development; the planned scenario was that women would sue state governments for denying their rights, not that voting women would be charged with a criminal offense. It seemed that the federal government was just as anxious to bring a test case as were the suffragists. Anthony hoped that even if the U.S. district court did not decide in her favor, she could take the case on appeal to the Supreme Court. That would be the chance for an authoritative decision on whether the right to vote was an inherent right of U.S. citizenship.

Anthony was convicted and fined $100. She refused to pay, but because the judge also refused to imprison her for nonpayment, she was left with no avenue through which to appeal to the Supreme Court. The case that became the test case was instead that of Virginia Minor, who together with her husband (as a married woman under Missouri law she could not bring a case alone) sued the state electoral officials who had refused to allow her to vote. Defeated in the state courts, the Minors took their appeal to the Supreme Court. The case, *Minor v. Happersett*, decided in 1875, turned on interpretation of the Fourteenth Amendment. By the time the Court ruled, the decision had already been determined by two other Fourteenth Amendment cases three years earlier: the so-called "Slaughterhouse cases," and *Bradwell v. Illinois*, in which Myra Bradwell charged that the refusal of the state of Illinois to let her practice law was a denial of her Fourteenth Amendment rights. In both cases the Supreme Court had ruled against the plaintiffs.

The denials made clear that the Court would insist on narrow interpretation of the Fourteenth Amendment, one that would leave as much leeway as possible to state's rights, and retreat from the assertion of national power and authority that the postwar period of constitutional creativity had seemed to usher in. The Fourteenth Amendment, the Court declared, was intended for the specific protection of freedmen and could not be construed to mean the wholesale transfer of issues of state citizenship to national authority. In 1875, in the *Minor* case, the Supreme Court added that suffrage was *not* a right inherent in citizenship and that the Constitution of the United States did not in fact enfranchise anyone. Who voted was a matter for the states to decide, and the Fifteenth Amendment merely laid down certain grounds that the states could *not* use for denying the vote to its citizens.

This decision was a major blow. It meant of course that the New Departure was no longer viable. It was also an authoritative denial of a democratic philosophical position held by many Americans, not only feminists, that participation in government was a natural right, logically prior to any particular government, confirmed by the state but not bestowed by it. Further, as Anthony realized, a narrow interpretation of the Fifteenth Amendment that saw it as merely prohibiting race and "previous condition of servitude" as grounds for denying the vote, opened the way for other, different grounds to be used with impunity. This was what happened by the turn of the century when Southern states managed to disfranchise most of their black male citizens without provoking constitutional rebuttal. The Fifteenth Amendment turned out to be not only of no help to women but a Pyrrhic victory for African-American men.

The Supreme Court's slamming the door on a Fourteenth Amendment route also meant the end of any claim to woman suffrage as an aspect of "universal" human rights, guaranteed to women as part of the whole American community. From now on the vote would have to be demanded as a specific grant to women as a class. Suffragists now had to rethink their political strategy.

One possible route to enfranchisement was to make it a thoroughly political question and convince one of the major parties to adopt woman suffrage as a party plank. Many New England men involved with the AWSA were hopeful about a Republican initiative, and Henry Blackwell made an all-out effort to gain an endorsement for the 1872 election. All he got was a lukewarm expression of general goodwill. As a strategy, the party-political route had even less chance of success than the New Departure. 1872 turned out to be the high point of Republican interest in woman suffrage. Thereafter it cooled rapidly.

Two years earlier, after the Fifteenth Amendment had been adopted and Hiram Revels, the first African-American senator, had taken his seat, Cady Stanton's son, Gerrit, had written to his sister: "I suppose mother and Susan think they come next. But they are doomed to disappointment. . . . Now, what party, to day, would be benefitted by Woman's Suffrage? Neither. Ergo, until something turns up whereby the life of one of the parties depends on the granting of Woman Suffrage, mother and Susan will have to stand outside and see *'us men'* run the machine." His mother actually printed this letter in the *Revolution*, with the editorial comment: "'Us men' have run the machine quite long enough, and we refuse to stand outside any longer." But her son was correct. While individual politicians, such as George Julian, were personally committed to woman suffrage and could be counted on to present petitions and speak to the subject in Congress, neither of the major parties found political advantage in making it party policy, as the Republicans had done with the Fourteenth and Fifteenth Amendments. The organized women's movement would have to grow far larger, and its nuisance value much greater, before it would force political parties to take it seriously.

This left the old state-by-state strategy of lobbying, petitioning, and agitating for grants of suffrage from state legislatures, along with attempts to short-circuit this approach via a Sixteenth Amendment declaring that the vote should not be denied on grounds of sex. Several states revised their constitutions in the 1870s, and in all of them, state woman suffrage associations geared themselves to agitate for a woman suffrage clause. Leaders of both the NWSA and the AWSA arrived to speak (usually at different times), and their presence generated flurries of enthusiasm. The campaigns also helped to keep women's suffrage societies alive and drew in new recruits. Nonetheless the result was a list of failures. Illinois and Colorado in 1870, Ohio in 1873, Michigan in 1874, California in 1878—all failed to give women the vote in their new constitutions. Other states saw woman suffrage bills introduced into the legislatures and predictably defeated, or not even making it to a vote. In Colorado a popular referendum in 1877, for which Stone, Blackwell, and Susan B. Anthony campaigned extensively, was heavily defeated. In the face of this dismal record, some state woman suffrage societies faded away; others struggled gamely on, not to experience much rejuvenation until the late 1880s.

Suffragists now had to cope with more vigorous opposition too. As the agitation for woman suffrage grew more insistent and visible, those who argued against it also became stronger, more theoretically grounded, and organized. The assumption that the vote was a badge of masculinity, part of a parcel of masculine prerogatives and duties, like the obligation to fight, was still very strong. Thus women's demands for it seemed to imply an attack on men. Any claim to share male authority was "neither more nor less than a challenge of the rights of masculinity," wrote theologian Horace Bushnell in 1869. A reporter for the *Chicago Inter-Ocean*, writing from Indian fighter George Custer's camp in 1874, put it more crudely: "If Susan B. Anthony wants to vote . . . let her take a scalp."

Bushnell's widely read book, *Women's Suffrage: The Reform Against Nature,* is as interesting for what it concedes as for its adamant opposition to women voting. It demonstrates the extent to which the whole question of women's role had developed by the end of the 1860s. Bushnell favored coeducation in colleges, and he wanted to see women in certain jobs that in fact they did not penetrate until well into the twentieth century. He thought women might be employed as hotel managers, bank tellers, insurance actuaries, brokers, physicians (though not surgeons), and in certain kinds of legal work— "the silent, in-door, office work"—not pleading in court; they might be college professors in such subjects as languages, botany, and exact mathematics. He suggested that the management of almshouses, hospitals, and common schools be taken out of state hands and given to private enterprise, particularly to women. But women should not meddle with anything that implied authority or rule in government.

Bushnell was also in the mainstream of much post–Civil War thinking that repudiated Lockean liberal ideas of individual rights and a compact theory of government in favor of a much more organic notion of the state and society. The enfranchisement of African-American men through the Fifteenth Amendment was the culmination and last gasp of that antebellum natural rights philosophy and idealism that had been the theoretical underpinning of women's rights advocacy. By the 1870s natural rights arguments were less effective in the general society, and so was the appeal of individualism. Increasingly the family, not the individual, was seen as the base unit of society, and defending the health of the family became the central theme in antifeminist rhetoric.

The implication here was that any movement that worked toward the individuality of the wife and gave her a role or interests apart from those of her husband, fatally weakened the family. However softened and disguised in practice, at bottom the family rested on the subordination of wife to husband. A strong unit had to be essentially patriarchal; thus feminism was defined as basically antifamily. The main objection to woman suffrage, wrote the Catholic journalist Orestes Brownson in 1869, was that it would "weaken and finally break up and destroy the Christian family" in a society that was already "rapidly becoming a nation of isolated individuals, without family ties or affections." An interesting curiosity was a petition to the Senate in 1874 suggesting that the vote be allowed only to married male householders over thirty. The petitioner protested that woman suffrage would break down the barriers between the spheres of men and women, in the process "virtually *destroying* woman's sphere." It was signed by Frances Guthrie d'Arusemont—the daughter of Frances Wright!

For the first time there appeared not just blank indifference or individual rebukes but *organized* antisuffragism among women. Prosuffrage petitions were now being met with *anti-suffrage* petitions signed by women. Two hundred women signed such a document in Massachusetts in 1868, asking not to have the vote "imposed" upon them since it could only bring discord into the family. Similar petitions appeared in Ohio. In the capital an Anti-Sixteenth Amendment Society was founded in 1870, led by the wife of Admiral Dahlgren, a number of other wives of prominent politicians, and the distinguished educator Almira Lincoln Phelps, sister of Emma Willard. The society produced a remonstrance to Congress, signed by five thousand women, including Catharine Beecher, to protest the extension of suffrage to women. Matilda Gage, on behalf of the NWSA, invited Mrs. Dahlgren to address their convention in 1872 to open up her position for debate, but she declined for reasons of "female modesty." Like the suffragists, the antis claimed they spoke for the mass of women; they were certainly used by male politicians to demonstrate that not only did most women not care about the vote, they were actually opposed to it. An antisuffrage petition with just under fourteen hundred female signatures was enough for the Illinois Constitutional Convention to decide not to include a woman suffrage clause or even put it to a popular vote.

The emergence of this kind of organized female opposition, and the persistence of arguments that pitted "the family" against the rights of women, forced feminists constantly to refute and counter them. In doing so they often fell into the trap of accepting their opponents' framing of the question, so that much of their energy was expended in insisting that they *did* believe in marriage and motherhood and were not attacking Christianity.

By the 1870s an ominous antifeminist intellectual attack was emerging from the direction of science. In 1876 Lucy Stone noted in the *Woman's Journal* that "the old opposition, founded on texts of Scripture, has ceased to be urged or nearly so; . . . the later form of scientific objection is now coolly affirmed." By the late 1860s an amalgam of evolutionist ideas, based on both Darwin and Herbert Spencer, was percolating through middle-class culture and came to underlie much of the late-nineteenth-century educated worldview. When applied to explaining differences between the sexes (and among races), Darwinism was used to provide a scientific gloss on common popular assumptions of superiority and inferiority. So powerful were evolutionist arguments that feminists felt compelled to refute them on their own terms. But this put them in the situation of accepting the idea that the equality of the sexes was to be decided by science and that equality of rights or the opening of opportunities had somehow to be related to demonstrating an equality in nature of "man" and "woman." This was a line of argument that before the war had seemed irrelevant to a movement focused on the self-development of the individual.

The most elaborate feminist effort to refute Darwin came from Antoinette Brown Blackwell. She had become increasingly interested in science and had taught herself enough to be able to make a respectable attack on the Darwinian idea that women were less fully evolved than men. In her 1876 book *The Sexes Throughout Nature* she denied that the male must be assumed to be the "representative type of the species." Blackwell, unlike Stanton and Anthony, had always believed in fundamental mental and psychological differences between the sexes. She accepted now that these differences had been produced by evolution, but she refused to concede that the differences could be hierarchically evaluated as superior and inferior. What she ended up with, however, sounded suspiciously like a scientific reworking of traditional ideas about separate but complementary characteristics and functions. She also accepted that it was to science "we must undoubtedly look for a final and authoritative decision as to woman's legitimate nature and functions."

The import of "science" for women was brought home in a very practical way in 1873 with the publication of *Sex in Education*, by Edward H. Clarke, a doctor who had been a professor at the Harvard Medical School. It was an enormously influential attack on coeducation, and in fact on higher academic education for girls altogether. With the misleading subtitle "A Fair Chance for Girls," Clarke's book conceded that young women students might be mentally capable of doing college-level work, but he insisted that the strain was physically devastating. Since a high school and college education took place during those adolescent years in which women's reproductive maturity was being established, the diversion of vital energy to the brain fatally weakened the female system. The result, he declared, was that the colleges were turning out a bunch of neurasthenic invalids who would never be able to become healthy mothers. The solution to "the problem of woman's sphere," he pointed out, indicating the way in which the question of women's rights was going to be hijacked by science, "is not to be solved by applying to it abstract principles of right and wrong. Its solution must be obtained from physiology."

Feminists of all stripes immediately saw the danger in

Clarke's book. Women's right to a higher education was, after all, a question which they had reason to think they were halfway to winning. Harvard and Yale might still be closed to women, but by 1870, 169 of America's 582 colleges and universities had become coeducational, and a real university-level college for women, Vassar, had been established in 1861. All the reports from these institutions, coeducational or single sex, indicated that women students not only could keep up with the work but were often among the top students. But were all these top students then going home to become nervous invalids? Was education ruining the potential mothers of America? The *Woman's Journal* immediately denounced the book, and Thomas Wentworth Higginson made a trip to Vassar to investigate. Other feminists busily collected statistics on the vibrant health of college girls, and Julia Ward Howe, now president of the AWSA, assembled a collection of essays by educational and feminist luminaries to refute Clarke point by point.

While feminist energies were being diverted to meet these kinds of unexpected challenges, a number of new organizations for women were being founded. In some ways they were part of a women's movement, but they also rivaled the suffrage organizations for the loyalty and energies of activist women. In 1868 Sorosis was founded, the first women's club and the forerunner of what would become an immensely influential women's club movement. The club movement was designed to provide a social space where educated and intelligent women could meet others like themselves while avoiding such controversial and radical questions as suffrage. Many educated women were attracted to the new American Social Science Association, which Caroline Dall helped to found in Boston in 1865, and to which she switched most of her energies.

In 1873 Sorosis members launched the nationwide Association for the Advancement of Women. Comprised of professional and elite women, it held yearly congresses where issues of interest to women, especially social reform questions, were discussed in both a Christian and a more modern "scientific" spirit. There was some overlap of membership with the woman suffrage movement—both Julia Ward Howe and Antoinette Brown Blackwell were active in the AAW—but it was created as an alternative to the suffrage organizations. It attracted women who were more comfortable with an organization focused on widening woman's sphere and working for social betterment than with the "selfish" demands of the suffrage movement. Howe described the speakers at its inaugural meeting as "true-hearted wives, mothers and maids whose eloquence was full of the spirit and sanctity of home."

A more dangerous rival for the loyalties of American women was the Women's Christian Temperance Union. It was founded in 1874 after an extraordinary outburst of direct action by women in Ohio and throughout the Midwest against the liquor industry. Groups of praying women descended on liquor stores and saloons, pleading with the owners to close shop. In several instances the women went beyond praying to smash up liquor stores. At least 56,000 and probably as many as 150,000 women were involved. Clearly this was a mass movement.

The leaders of the suffrage movement were taken by surprise and did not quite know what to make of all this sudden radical activity by apparently ordinary housewives. Cady Stanton found the whole affair rather disreputable; she did not approve of the destruction of property, and she realized that though these women's *actions* might be radical, their basic ideology had little to do with feminism as she understood it. The so-called women's crusade waned after about six months, but out of it came a permanent organization, the Women's Christian Temperance Union, which grew with extraordinary rapidity. By 1890 it already had 160,000 members—numbers that the suffrage organizations could come nowhere near matching.

Henry Blackwell was bewildered that the WCTU would not come out in favor of the ballot in spite of its boldness in so many other ways: "That women who are too conservative or too timid to desire a voice in the making of the laws which govern them," he wrote, "should have been moved to so marked a departure from the old paths, is to us, we confess, a puzzling enigma." But as Cady Stanton had perceived, the WCTU women were on a different trajectory: they were not acting radically to break out of their sphere, they were acting radically to protect it. They were not rebelling at their domestic confinement, they were protesting that men, through the abuse of liquor, were failing to protect and sustain women's sphere. The motto of the association was "Home Protection."

Thus by the mid-1870s many fresh voices were claiming to speak for women and offering new avenues of expression and association. Many state suffrage associations found their membership drained away by these other attractions. The activity of both the NWSA and the AWSA declined after 1875 and did not intensify again until they merged in 1890. By the late 1870s, the lessons that suffragists could draw from developments since the Civil War were rather bitter. They had learned that their concerns were considered peripheral to the great constitutional developments of the age. They had learned that any hint of sexual impropriety or deviancy could send many fringe supporters running for cover. Now they were learning that when it came to moving women in new directions, the suffrage movement was not the only game in town. The formidable task that lay ahead was to recapture the initiative and make the suffrage movement the core and focal point of the movement of women.

Meanwhile the doldrums of the late 1870s and 1880s had to be weathered. It is a tribute to the dedication and stamina of the leaders of both the NWSA and the AWSA that they kept both these national societies in existence, lectured and wrote, lobbied and petitioned, kept an eye out for every opportunity to press women's claims, and, indefatigably year after year, kept the cause alive.

7

Centennial: The Women's Movement in 1876

AFTER A PERIOD of generally declining momentum for the women's movement in the late 1870s and 1880s, the two national associations, the NWSA and the AWSA, in 1890 reconciled and agreed to merge. Although Susan B. Anthony dominated the new association, the merger was essentially on AWSA terms—that is, a strict and narrow concentration on gaining the ballot, with no distractions of "side issues." In fact by 1890 Anthony had come to accept that this was the only possible route to follow. Concentrating on the suffrage goal at all costs meant, among other things, a strong effort to win the participation of Southern white women, and thus a readiness by organization leaders to acquiesce in Southern demands that the movement segregate its black members. Even this capitulation to bigotry and discrimination did not hasten success. Not until 1920, seventy-two years after the Seneca Falls convention, did the Nineteenth Amendment to the Constitution remove sex as a bar to exercising the vote. By this time a number of individual states had already granted the ballot, including the populous states of California in 1911 and New York in 1917. By the time the Nineteenth Amendment was ratified, almost all the major leaders who had carried the movement for so long were dead. Only Antoinette Brown Blackwell lived to cast her first vote at the age of ninety-six, as did the only surviving member of the Seneca Falls convention, the rebellious glovemaker Charlotte Woodward.

By this time, too, other parts of the world had not only caught up with the United States in the matter of woman suffrage but had forged ahead. New Zealand women had received the vote in 1893; Australians in 1902; Finnish and Norwegian women in 1906 and 1907; women in Canada and Britain in 1918. This was not because the women's movement in these countries was necessarily stronger than in the United States (with the possible exception of Britain, quite the contrary) but because conservative opposition was much weaker, and because the structure of government made decisive social change of this kind easier.

But in 1876, as the nation prepared to celebrate the anniversary of its independence, and suffragists debated how best to mark the occasion, they knew none of this. They had been working for women's rights for twenty-eight years, and they had always known it would be a long haul; they probably did not anticipate another thirty-four years. Cady Stanton was now sixty, Anthony fifty-six, and Lucy Stone fifty-eight. Some of their old comrades had departed the field. Lucretia Mott was eighty and frail; Harriot Hunt had died in 1875; Paulina Wright Davis was to die in August 1876; Ernestine Rose had retired to England; Frances Gage was bedridden. But Cady Stanton, Anthony, and Stone would all three continue active in the movement well into their eighties.

Many states had already made significant improvements in the legal status of married women, and that trend would continue; two territories had granted women the vote; three states allowed women to vote for school boards. Otherwise there had been little success on the suffrage front. But it was the growth of opportunities for women to lead fuller and more in-dependent lives that had always been the major goal of the movement, not the ballot alone.

Cady Stanton in 1869 had exhorted: "We must stir up the girls everywhere to crowd into the colleges and professions, profitable trades and political offices, and thus decrease the supply of laborers for schools and sewing machines, and thereby raise the wages of all." Young women were still flock-ing to be schoolteachers, and working in the sewing trades, but as the 1870 Census revealed, among the one in eight women over age ten who were gainfully employed, at least a few were to be found in practically every one of the occupa-tions listed in the census. In 1863 a woman named Virginia Penny had published *How Women Can Make Money*, an "en-cyclopedia" of jobs that women could, and were, doing, com-plete with a range of wages, working conditions, general availability, and so on, based on extensive research. The book made little impact at the time, but after its reissue in 1870 it was an instant success and went into several editions over the next fourteen years. Young women in "white collar" jobs in cities, businesswomen, women journalists or doctors or even ministers were still a small minority of American women, but they were no longer such a total novelty as before the war.

Nor was the female college graduate. Vassar College, opened in 1865, had now been joined by Wellesley and Smith colleges. A number of state universities had become coeduca-tional, less from commitment to the equality of women than from the realization that fees paid for a daughter were worth as much as fees paid for a son—but coeducational nonetheless. Women assuming the authority to speak from a public plat-form were no longer an occasion for amazement and ridicule. All these developments might give cause for cautious opti-mism.

Still, the strongest feeling of suffragists as the nation prepared for its centennial celebrations was anger. Not only did they feel that *they* had not achieved liberty, equality, and independence in 1776, but the authorities in charge of the Centennial International Exhibition in Philadelphia, which would showcase the accomplishments of the nation, had made no effort to provide space or attention for women's achievements. A Woman's Pavilion was planned, but only because the specially selected conservative women appointed as fund-raisers for the exhibition took the initiative to collect extra money to erect their own space. The male authorities clearly saw the celebrations as a purely masculine affair. Lucy Stone was so angry that her first impulse was to boycott the centennial celebrations entirely and advise all women to do the same. Indeed, she suggested they might try dressing in mourning on July 4 as a symbol of their own lack of rights. Eventually she relented and prepared an exhibit illustrating various attempts made by women to protest "Taxation Without Representation." She sent it off to the Woman's Pavilion in Philadelphia, where it was hung in an obscure spot where it was virtually unreadable.

Cady Stanton was also lukewarm about participating, but Anthony and some of the younger NWSA women felt that some feminist statement must be made at the main celebrations. Denied the use of a major hall, Matilda Joslyn Gage managed to rent a suite of rooms in a house and set up a suffrage parlor, filled with pamphlets and information, where visiting sympathizers could drop by, chat, and sign the visitors' book. But the main event was to be the presentation of the women's own Declaration of Rights for Women, worked up by Cady Stanton and Gage. The declaration was available to be signed in the NWSA parlor, and hundreds of women signed it, including ninety-four African-American women from Washington, D.C. It was printed and copies mailed all over the country. But Anthony wished to present the declaration at the official opening ceremonies of the exhibition in order that it might become part of the historic record of that day, demonstrating for "the daughters of 1976, the fact that their mothers of 1876 had thus asserted their equality of rights." She was willing to settle for a silent presentation, but when the authorities denied her permission even for that, she and Gage, with three others, decided to crash the opening ceremonies.

On July 4, immediately after the Declaration of Independence had been read, the five women marched quickly up to the platform in Independence Hall and presented the startled presiding officer with a three-foot-long parchment scroll of their own declaration. "Mr. President, we present this Declaration of Rights of the women citizens of the United States," said Susan B. Anthony, and the five then exited as smartly as they had arrived, handing out copies of the document as they left. Outside, Anthony read the declaration to a large enthusiastic crowd. Though Lucy Stone had had no part in preparing the document, when she read it later she approved, and did not even condemn the brash method of its presentation. She had dreaded to think what Cady Stanton and Anthony might decide to do in Philadelphia; but, she wrote to a friend, "they seem to be on good behavior."

This declaration is less pithy than the 1848 Declaration of Sentiments, and the wrongs complained of are cast in less religious and more strictly constitutional terms. Instead of accusing "men" it "impeached" the government for violating the rights of American women: by denying them representation in government; by taxing them without representation; by denying women the right of trial by jury of their peers; by subjecting women to an "aristocracy of sex" through universal *male* suffrage. The formulation reflected the turn toward political and constitutional thinking that had developed since the Civil War. Other specific complaints reflected the issues with which the movement had been grappling through the last twenty-eight years—the unequal laws governing the sexual conduct of men and women, and the remaining legal disabilities of married women.

The document was in many ways a fitting closure to the first phase of the women's movement. In its opening reaffirmation of the natural and equal rights of each individual, and in a ringing closing peroration, the declaration summed up a universalist feminist philosophy based on natural human rights, the most essential of which was the liberty necessary for full individual development. This was a philosophy that had sustained the movement since its inception. In the years to come it would be overlaid with appeals to the special virtue of women and with claims to political power based on the role of women as mothers and the practical social reforms that voting women would effect. In its origins, however, the women's movement had never been entirely, or even mainly, about the achievement of specific "reforms"; it was essentially about new ways of being a woman. It was a *movement* of women toward an open-ended vision of emancipation, and was in itself emancipatory.

"And now, at the close of a hundred years," the declaration ended,

> as the hour-hand of the great clock that marks the centuries points to 1876, we declare our faith in the principles of self-government; our full equality with man in natural rights; that woman was made first for her own happiness, with the absolute right to herself—to all the opportunities and advantages life affords for her complete development; and we deny that dogma of the centuries, incorporated in the codes

of all nations—that woman was made for man—her best
interests, in all cases, to be sacrificed to his will. We ask of
our rulers, at this hour, no special favors, no special privileges, no special legislation. We ask justice, we ask equality,
we ask that all the civil and political rights that belong to
citizens of the United States, be guaranteed to us and our
daughters for ever.

A Note on Sources

There is no substitute for reading the words of the historical actors themselves. Fortunately the early-nineteenth-century feminists are not only very readable, but many of their speeches, writings, and letters are easily accessible. The *Papers of Elizabeth Cady Stanton and Susan B. Anthony*, edited by Patricia G. Holland and Ann D. Gordon, are available on microfilm in forty-five reels (Scholarly Resources, Inc., 1992). These contain not only the correspondence of the two women but manuscript diaries and speeches, newspaper clippings, and complete files of the *Revolution*. The papers of Isabella Beecher Hooker have also been microfilmed by the Stowe-Day Foundation in Hartford, Conn., and an introduction to the project by Anne Throne Margolis is published separately (Hartford, Conn., 1979).

More comfortable to read are several good collections of printed documents. Short extracts from the antebellum women's press can be found in Ann Russo and Cheris Kramarae, *The Radical Women's Press of the 1850s* (New York, 1991); and selections from the *Revolution* in Lana Rakow and Cheris Kramarae, eds., *The Revolution in Words: Righting Women, 1868–1871* (New York, 1990). A number of documentary collections cover the early years of the women's rights movement. Among the best are Elizabeth Frost and Kathryn Cullen-Dupont, *Women's Suffrage in America: An Eyewitness History* (New York, 1992), and Ruth Barnes Moynihan, et al., eds., *Second to None: A Documentary History of American Women*, 2 vols. (Lincoln, Nebr., 1993). Virginia Bernhard and Elizabeth Fox-Genovese, eds., *The Birth of American Feminism: The Seneca Falls Woman's Convention of 1848*

(New York, 1995) contains longer selections from various women's rights conventions of the 1850s and from the women's press, as well as documents pertinent to Seneca Falls. Alice S. Rossi, *The Feminist Papers: From Adams to de Beauvoir* (New York, 1973) is a superior collection with long selections and excellent commentary. *Elizabeth Cady Stanton/Susan B. Anthony: Correspondence, Writings, Speeches,* edited by Ellen DuBois (rev. ed., New York, 1992), has a fine introduction.

Cady Stanton's autobiography, *Eighty Years and More* (New York, 1898; reprinted New York, 1971), is lively reading. So are Harriot Hunt's memoirs, *Glances and Glimpses: Or Fifty Years Social, Including Twenty Years Professional, Life* (1856, reprinted New York, 1970). Karlyn Kohrs Campbell, *Man Cannot Speak for Her,* 2 vols. (New York, 1989), reproduces a number of speeches and analyzes women's rights rhetoric. Beth M. Waggenspach, *The Search for Self-Sovereignty* (Westport, Conn., 1989) reprints some of Cady Stanton's major speeches, with commentary. The correspondence of Lucy Stone and Henry Blackwell is collected in Leslie Wheeler, ed., *Loving Warriors; Selected Letters of Lucy Stone and Henry B. Blackwell, 1853–1893* (New York, 1981), and that between Stone and Antoinette Brown Blackwell in Carol Lasser and Marlene Deahl Merrill, *Friends and Sisters: Letters Between Lucy Stone and Antoinette Brown Blackwell, 1846–93* (Urbana, Ill., 1987); both books have good commentaries and annotations. Larry Ceplair, ed., *The Public Years of Sarah and Angelina Grimké: Selected Writings, 1835–1839* (New York, 1989) reprints the sisters' writings with good commentary. Dorothy Sterling, *We Are Your Sisters: Black Women in the 19th Century* (New York, 1984) contains documents on some African-American feminists.

The basic documentary collection is the three-volume *History of Woman Suffrage,* compiled by Elizabeth Cady Stanton, Susan B. Anthony, and Matilda Joslyn Gage in 1881 (reprinted Salem, N.H., 1985). It is infuriating to use, because it is literally a compilation of speeches, convention proceedings, letters, reminiscences of participants, and newspaper clippings, organized mainly by state rather than theme or strict chronology, and there is no index. But dipping into it can be quite engrossing. A one-volume *Concise History of Woman Suffrage* is edited by Mari Jo and Paul Buhle (Urbana, Ill., 1978). Philip S. Foner, ed., *The Factory Girls* (Urbana, Ill., 1977) is an indispensable documentary source for the attitudes of wage-earning women. Jeanne Boydston, Mary Kelley, and Anne Margolis, *The Limits of Sisterhood: The Beecher Sisters on Women's Rights and Woman's Sphere* (Chapel Hill, 1988) is a fascinating collection of the sisters' letters and writings, with excellent commentary, placing them both in their society and their family. Other interesting short printed documents are: Gerda Lerner, ed., "Sarah M. Grimké's 'Sisters of Charity,'" *Signs*, 1 (1975), 216–256, and Lerner's update in "Comment," *Signs*, 10 (1985), 811–815; and Ellen DuBois, ed., "On Labor and Free Love: Two Unpublished Speeches of Elizabeth Cady Stanton," *Signs*, 1 (1975), 257–268. The schoolgirl correspondence of Caroline Healey and Ednah Cheney is in Margaret McFadden, "Boston Teenagers Debate the Woman Question, 1837–1838," *Signs*, 15 (1990), 832–846. For the writings of the male feminists, see Michael S. Kimmel and Thomas E. Mosmiller, eds., *Against the Tide: Pro-Feminist Men in the United States, 1776–1990* (Boston, 1992), and Philip S. Foner, ed., *Frederick Douglass on Women's Rights* (Westport, Conn., 1976). Windsor Daggett, *A Down East Yankee from the District of Maine* (Portland, Me., 1920) reprints some of John Neal's speeches and writings on women. The remark at the end of Chapter 1 is quoted in Nancy Coffey Heffernan and Ann Page Stecker, *Sisters of Fortune* (Amherst, Mass., 1993). The quotation from Caroline Dall on page 94 is from her *Historical Pictures Retouched* (Boston, 1860).

SECONDARY SOURCES

An indispensable reference work is Edward T. James, ed., *Notable American Women: A Biographical Dictionary, 1607–1950,*

3 vols. (Cambridge, Mass., 1971). The standard work on the entire women's rights movement up to the achievement of suffrage in 1920 is Eleanor Flexner's classic *Century of Struggle* (New York, 1959, enlarged rev. ed., with Ellen Fitzpatrick, Cambridge, Mass., 1996). Nancy Woloch's sophisticated text, *Women and the American Experience* (rev. ed., New York, 1994) has two excellent chapters on the movement. My discussion of how social movements are organized and grow is taken from Steven M. Buechler, *Women's Movements in the United States: Woman Suffrage, Equal Rights, and Beyond* (New Brunswick, N.J., 1990) and from Brenda Diana Phillips, "The Decade of Origin: Resource Mobilization and Women's Rights in the 1850s," Ph.D. dissertation, Ohio State University, 1985. See also Buechler's *Transformation of the Woman Suffrage Movement: The Case of Illinois, 1850–1920* (New Brunswick, N.J., 1986), an illuminating case study. Keith E. Melder, *Beginnings of Sisterhood: The American Woman's Rights Movement, 1800–1850* (New York, 1977) has a fine account of the developments up to 1850 that rightly stresses the importance of the 1840s. Miriam Gurko's *The Ladies of Seneca Falls: The Birth of the Woman's Rights Movement* (New York, 1974) is a lively and readable account. The essays in Marjorie Spruill Wheeler, ed., *One Woman, One Vote: Rediscovering the Woman Suffrage Movement* (Troutdale, Ore., 1995) deal with various aspects of the suffrage movement up to 1920.

Several good modern biographies of the major leaders are available. Cady Stanton has two: Elisabeth Griffith, *In Her Own Right: The Life of Elizabeth Cady Stanton* (New York, 1984) and Lois W. Banner, *Elizabeth Cady Stanton: A Radical for Woman's Rights* (Boston, 1980). Kathleen Barry, *Susan B. Anthony: A Biography of a Singular Feminist* (New York, 1988) is a sympathetic and imaginative account, with an interesting theoretical post-script on the writing of women's biography. The older Ida Husted Harper, *Life and Work of Susan B. Anthony*, 2 vols. (1898, reprinted Salem, N.H., 1983) contains copies of no-longer-extant letters and some of Anthony's speeches. Elizabeth Cazden, *Antoinette Brown Blackwell: A Biography* (Old Westbury, N.Y., 1983) is a fine biography of a feminist who deserves to be better known; Andrea Moore Kerr, *Lucy Stone: Speaking Out for Equality* (New Brunswick, N.J., 1992) is also an excellent study. Much less information is available on the interesting Ernestine Rose. Yuri Suhl's *Ernestine L. Rose: Women's Rights Pioneer* (2nd ed., New York, 1990) is a reissue of the original 1959 work with an introduction by Françoise Basch, and includes extracts from some of Rose's speeches. Lucretia Mott has a good biographer in Margaret Hope Bacon, *Valiant Friend: The Life of Lucretia Mott* (New York, 1980). For Frances Wright, see Celia Morris Eckhardt, *Frances Wright: Rebel in America* (Cambridge, Mass., 1984); Carol A. Kolmerten, *Women in Utopia: The Ideology of Gender in the American Owenite Communities* (Bloomington, Ind., 1990); and Lori D. Ginzberg, "'The Hearts of Your Readers Will Shudder': Fanny Wright, Infidelity, and American Freethought," *American Quarterly*, 46 (June 1994), 195–226. The literature on Margaret Fuller is massive. Among the best works are Charles Capper, *Margaret Fuller: An American Romantic Life* (New York, 1992), vol. 1: *The Private Years*; Mary Kelley, ed., *The Portable Margaret Fuller* (New York, 1994), with an excellent introduction; Christina Zwarg, *Feminist Conversations: Fuller, Emerson and the Play of Reading* (Ithaca, N.Y., 1995); Julie Ellison, *Delicate Subjects* (Ithaca, N.Y., 1990); Elaine Showalter, "Miranda and Cassandra: The Discourse of the Feminist Intellectual," in Florence Howe, ed., *Tradition and the Talents of Women* (Urbana, Ill., 1991); and Eve Kornfeldt, *Margaret Fuller; A Brief Biography with Documents* (Boston, 1996). For the Grimké sisters, see Gerda Lerner, *The Grimké Sisters from South Carolina: Rebels Against Slavery* (Boston, 1967), and the very perceptive Katherine Du Pré Lumpkin, *The Emancipation of Angelina Grimké* (Chapel Hill, 1974). For Victoria Woodhull, see Lois B. Underhill, *The Woman Who Ran for President: The Many Lives of Victoria Woodhull* (Bridgehampton, N.Y., 1995) and Madeleine B. Stern, *The Victoria*

Woodhull Reader (Weston, Mass., 1974). Mary H. Grant, *Julia Ward Howe: Private Woman, Public Person* (New York, 1994) is a modern biography of one of the important "new" feminists of the postwar period.

On international comparisons, see Christine Bolt, *The Women's Movements in the United States and Britain from the 1790s to the 1920s* (Amherst, Mass., 1993), and Jane Rendall, *The Origins of Modern Feminism: Women in Britain, France and the United States, 1780–1860* (Basingstoke, England, 1985). Elizabeth K. Helsinger, Robin Lauterbach Sheets, and William Veeder, eds., *The Woman Question: Society and Literature in Britain and America, 1837–1883*, 3 vols. (Chicago, 1983) is a fascinating combination of commentary and long extracts from British and American writings on various aspects of the Woman Question.

INTERPRETIVE STUDIES

Nancy Cott, *The Bonds of Womanhood: "Woman's Sphere" in New England, 1780–1835* (New Haven, 1977) is the classic discussion of the development of "woman's sphere" and its relation with feminism. Judith Wellman, "The Seneca Falls Women's Rights Convention: A Study of Social Networks," *Journal of Women's History*, 3 (Spring 1991), 9–37, analyzes the signers of the Declaration of Sentiments. The rhetoric and philosophy of the nineteenth-century movement has been examined with insight by Sylvia D. Hoffert, *When Hens Crow: The Woman's Rights Movement in Antebellum America* (Bloomington, Ind., 1995) and Charles Conrad, "The Transformation of the 'Old Feminist' Movement," *Quarterly Journal of Speech*, 67 (1981), 284–297. Elizabeth Ann Bartlett, *Liberty, Equality, Sorority* (New York, 1994) discusses the thought of the Grimké sisters as well as Frances Wright and Margaret Fuller. Blanche Glassman Hersh, *The Slavery of Sex: Feminist-Abolitionists in America* (Urbana, Ill., 1978) has a particularly innovative chapter on feminist marriages. Susan Phinney Conrad, *Perish the Thought: Intellectual Women in Romantic*

America, 1830–1860 (New York, 1976) is a fine piece of intellectual history, as is Mary Kelley, *Private Woman, Public Stage: Literary Domesticity in Nineteenth-Century America* (New York, 1984). Linda Kerber, "Can a Woman Be an Individual? The Discourse of Self-Reliance," in Richard O. Curry and Lawrence B. Goodheart, eds., *American Chameleon: Individualism in Trans-National Context* (Kent, Ohio, 1991) and Mary G. Dietz, "Context Is All: Feminism and Theories of Citizenship," in Jill K. Conway, ed., *Learning About Women* (Ann Arbor, 1989) both ably discuss theories of liberal individualism and some current feminist criticisms of that tradition. Josephine Donovan, *Feminist Theory* (New York, 1985) analyzes nineteenth- and early-twentieth-century feminist thought. Elizabeth B. Clark, "Religion, Rights, and Difference in the Early Woman's Rights Movement," *Wisconsin Women's Law Journal*, 3 (1987), 29–58, is a subtle analysis. For the ideas of Caroline Dall, see Howard M. Wach, "A Boston Feminist in the Victorian Public Sphere: The Social Criticism of Caroline Healey Dall," *New England Quarterly*, 68 (1995), 429–450. I have dealt with various aspects of feminist thinking in the antebellum period in Jean V. Matthews, "Race, Sex, and the Dimensions of Liberty in Antebellum America," *Journal of the Early Republic*, 6 (Fall 1986), 274–291; and "Consciousness of Self and Consciousness of Sex in Antebellum Feminism," *Journal of Women's History*, 5 (Spring 1993), 61–78.

On education, see David F. Allemendinger, Jr., "Mount Holyoke Students Encounter the Need for Life-Planning, 1837–1850," *History of Education Quarterly*, 19 (Spring 1979), 27–46; Joan M. Jensen, "Not Only Ours But Others," *History of Education Quarterly*, 24 (Spring 1984), 3–19; Anne Firor Scott, *Making the Invisible Woman Visible* (Urbana, Ill., 1984); and Barbara Miller Solomon, *In the Company of Educated Women* (New Haven, Conn., 1985).

For the connection with the abolition movement, see Ellen Carol DuBois, "Women's Rights and Abolition: The Nature of the Connection," in Lewis Perry and Michael Fellman, eds., *Anti-Slavery Reconsidered* (Baton Rouge, 1979), 238–251. Kathryn Kish Sklar's penetrating essay, "'Women Who Speak for an Entire Nation': American and British Women at the World Anti-Slavery Convention, London, 1840," in Jean Fagan Yellin and John C. Van Horne, eds., *The Abolitionist Sisterhood: Women's Political Culture in Antebellum America* (Ithaca, N.Y., 1994), situates the activities of women abolitionists in the wider political culture of their respective nations.

On the relation with other reform movements, see Nancy A. Hewitt, *Women's Activism and Social Change: Rochester, New York, 1822–1872* (Ithaca, N.Y., 1984); Anne M. Boylan, "Women in Groups: An Analysis of Women's Benevolent Organizations in New York and Boston, 1797–1840," *Journal of American History*, 71 (December 1984), 497–515; Lori D. Ginzberg, *Women and the Work of Benevolence: Morality, Politics, and Class in the 19th-Century United States* (New Haven, Conn., 1990); and Barbara J. Berg, *The Remembered Gate: Origins of American Feminism, the Woman and the City, 1800–1860* (New York, 1978). For the connection with spiritualism, see Ann Braude's fine *Radical Spirits: Spiritualism and Women's Rights in Nineteenth-Century America* (Boston, 1989).

On marriage, see Elizabeth B. Clark, "Matrimonial Bonds: Slavery, Contract, and Divorce in Nineteenth-Century America," *Law and History Review*, 8 (Spring 1990), 25–54; Françoise Basch, "Women's Rights and the Wrongs of Marriage in Mid-Nineteenth-Century America," *History Workshop*, Autumn 1986, 18–40; and Amy Dru Stanley, "Conjugal Bonds and Wage Labor: Rights of Contract in the Age of Emancipation," *Journal of American History*, 75 (September 1988), 471–500. For legal developments concerning the rights of married women, see Norma Basch, *In the Eyes of the Law: Women, Marriage, and Property in Nineteenth-Century New York* (Ithaca, N.Y., 1982) and Elizabeth Bowles Warbasse, *The Changing Legal Rights of Married Women, 1800–1861* (New York, 1987).

For debates on divorce in the nineteenth century, see Glenda Riley, *Divorce: An American Tradition* (New York, 1991) and Nelson Manfred Blake, *The Road to Reno: A History of Divorce in the United States* (New York, 1962). On the "Free Love Counter Culture," see John C. Spurlock, *Free Love: Marriage and Middle-Class Radicalism in America, 1825–1860* (New York, 1988).

The women's rights press is dealt with in Martha M. Solomon, ed., *A Voice of Their Own: The Woman Suffrage Press, 1840–1910* (Tuscaloosa, Ala., 1991).

For Western suffrage developments, see Beverly Beeton, *Women Vote in the West: The Woman Suffrage Movement, 1869–1896* (New York, 1980). Also useful and interesting is Louise R. Noun, *Strong-Minded Women: The Emergence of the Woman-Suffrage Movement in Iowa* (Ames, Ia., 1969).

Material on the involvement of African-American women with the suffrage movement is more plentiful for the late nineteenth century than for the earlier period, but I found the following useful: Barbara Hilkert Andolsen, *"Daughters of Jefferson, Daughters of Bootblacks": Racism and American Feminism* (Macon, Ga., 1984); Rosalyn Terborg-Penn, *The Afro-American Woman* (Port Washington, N.Y., 1978); Nancy Caraway, *Segregated Sisterhood: Racism and the Politics of American Feminism* (Knoxville, Tenn., 1991); Carla L. Peterson, *Doers of the Word: African-American Speakers and Writers in the North, 1830–1880* (New York, 1995); and Paula Giddings, *When and Where I Enter: The Impact of Black Women on Race and Sex in America* (New York, 1984). Frances Watkins Harper is attracting more scholarly attention. I found Melba Joyce Boyd, *Discarded Legacy: Politics and Poetics in the Life of Frances Ellen Watkins Harper, 1825–1911* (Detroit, 1994) very perceptive. See also Frances Smith Foster, ed., *A Brighter Coming Day: A Frances Ellen Watkins Harper Reader* (New York, 1990) and Margaret Hope Bacon, "One Great Bundle of Humanity: Frances Ellen Watkins Harper (1825–1911)," *Pennsylvania Magazine of History and Biography*, January 1989, 21–43. *The Abolitionist Sisterhood*, cited above, contains two good essays on African-American women by Nell Irvin Painter and Carolyn Williams.

For women's role in the political culture of the United States, see Mary P. Ryan, *Women in Public: Between Banners and Ballots, 1825–1880* (Baltimore, 1990); Glenna Mathews, *The Rise of Public Woman* (New York, 1992); and Lori D. Ginzberg, "'Moral Suasion Is Moral Balderdash': Women, Politics, and Social Activism in the 1850s," *Journal of American History*, 73 (December 1986), 601–622. For the ideas of Habermas and their utility for feminism, see especially the essays in Craig Calhoun, ed., *Habermas and the Public Sphere* (Cambridge, Mass., 1992).

On questions of women's health care and birth control, see Jane B. Donegan, *'Hydropathic Highway to Health': Women and Water-cure in Antebellum America* (New York, 1986); Janet Farrell Brodie, *Contraception and Abortion in 19th Century America* (Ithaca, N.Y., 1994); and Linda Gordon, *Woman's Body, Woman's Right: A Social History of Birth Control in America* (New York, 1976).

For the antifeminists, see Kathryn Kish Sklar, *Catharine Beecher; A Study in American Domesticity* (New York, 1973), a classic study. Richard C. Lounsbury, ed., *Louisa S. McCord: Political and Social Essays* (Charlottesville, Va., 1995) reprints her essays denouncing feminism and has a good introduction. Horace Bushnell, *Woman Suffrage: The Reform Against Nature* (Boston, 1869) is a good example of "moderate" antisuffragism. Patricia Okker, *Our Sister Editors: Sarah J. Hale and the Tradition of Nineteenth-Century American Women Editors* (Athens, Ga., 1995) is a good interpretive discussion of Hale. Frances B. Cogan, *All-American Girl: The Ideal of Real Womanhood in Mid-Nineteenth-Century America* (Athens, Ga., 1989) is an innovative approach to a strand of thinking about women different from both extreme domesticity and feminism.

For Civil War developments, see Elizabeth D. Leonard, *Yankee Women: Gender Battles in the Civil War* (New York, 1994). Wendy Hammand Venet discusses the National Loyal League in some detail in *Neither Ballots nor Bullets: Woman Abolitionists and the Civil War* (Charlottesville, Va., 1991).

For post–Civil War developments, see Ellen Carol DuBois, *Feminism and Suffrage: The Emergence of an Independent Women's Movement in America, 1848–1869* (Ithaca, N.Y., 1978), which has become the standard account of the breakup of the old abolitionist-feminist alliance over the issue of the Fourteenth and Fifteenth Amendments. Israel Kugler, *From Ladies to Women: The Organized Struggle for Women's Rights in the Reconstruction Era* (New York, 1987) emphasizes relations with labor. William Leach's *True Love and Perfect Union: The Feminist Reform of Sex and Society* (New York, 1980) is a dense, brilliant examination of a wide range of feminist thinking in the postwar era, particularly as it converged upon a "social science world view." Karen J. Blair, *The Clubwoman as Feminist* (New York, 1980) discusses the creation of Sorosis and other women's organizations. Jack S. Blocker, Jr., "Separate Paths: Suffragists and the Women's Temperance Crusade," *Signs*, 10 (1985), 460–476, analyzes the response of suffragists to the Temperance crusade. Sally Roesch Wagner, *A Time of Protest: Suffragists Challenge the Republic, 1870–1887* (Sacramento, Calif., 1987) has a lively account of the feminist intervention at the 1876 Centennial Exhibition.

Two excellent articles on the constitutional ramifications of the Reconstruction period for woman suffrage are Ellen Carol DuBois, "Outgrowing the Compact of the Fathers: Equal Rights, Woman Suffrage, and the United States Constitution, 1820–1878," *Journal of American History*, 74 (December 1987), 836–862, and "Taking the Law into Our Own Hands: Bradwell, Minor, and Suffrage Militance in the 1870s," in Nancy Hewitt and Susan Lesock, eds., *Visible Women* (Urbana, Ill., 1993). On the important *Minor v. Happersett* case, see Norma Basch, "Reconstructing Female Citizenship," in Donald G. Nieman, ed., *The Constitution, Law, and American Life: Critical Aspects of the Nineteenth-Century Experience* (Athens, Ga., 1992).

Appendix:
Declaration of Sentiments, 1848

WHEN, in the course of human events, it becomes necessary for one portion of the family of man to assume among the people of the earth a position different from that which they have hitherto occupied, but one to which the laws of nature and of nature's God entitle them, a decent respect to the opinions of mankind requires that they should declare the causes that impel them to such a course.

We hold these truths to be self-evident: that all men and women are created equal; that they are endowed by their Creator with certain inalienable rights; that among these are life, liberty, and the pursuit of happiness; that to secure these rights governments are instituted, deriving their just powers from the consent of the governed. Whenever any form of Government becomes destructive of these ends, it is the right of those who suffer from it to refuse allegiance to it, and to insist upon the institution of a new government, laying its foundation on such principles, and organizing its powers in such form, as to them shall seem most likely to effect their safety and happiness. Prudence, indeed, will dictate that governments long established should not be changed for light and transient causes; and accordingly all experience hath shown that mankind are more disposed to suffer, while evils are sufferable, than to right themselves by abolishing the forms to which they were accustomed. But when a long train of abuses and usurpations, pursuing invariably the same object, evinces a design to reduce them under absolute despotism, it is their duty to throw off such government, and to provide new guards for their future security. Such has been the patient sufferance of the women under this government, and such is now the necessity which constrains them to demand the equal station to which they are entitled.

The history of mankind is a history of repeated injuries and usurpations on the part of man toward woman, having in direct object the establishment of an absolute tyranny over her. To prove this, let facts be submitted to a candid world.

He has never permitted her to exercise her inalienable right to the elective franchise.

He has compelled her to submit to laws, in the formation of which she had no voice.

He has withheld from her rights which are given to the most ignorant and degraded men—both natives and foreigners.

Having deprived her of this first right of a citizen, the elective franchise, thereby leaving her without representation in the halls of legislation, he has oppressed her on all sides.

He has made her, if married, in the eye of the law, civilly dead.

He has taken from her all right in property, even to the wages she earns.

He has made her, morally, an irresponsible being, as she can commit many crimes with impunity, provided they be done in the presence of her husband. In the covenant of marriage, she is compelled to promise obedience to her husband, he becoming to all intents and purposes, her master—the law giving him power to deprive her of her liberty, and to administer chastisement.

He has so framed the laws of divorce, as to what shall be the proper causes of divorce, and in case of separation, to whom the guardianship of the children shall be given, as to be wholly regardless of the happiness of women—the law, in all cases, going upon a false supposition of the supremacy of man, and giving all power into his hands.

After depriving her of all rights as a married woman, if single and the owner of property, he has taxed her to support a government which recognizes her only when her property can be made profitable to it.

He has monopolized nearly all the profitable employments, and from those she is permitted to follow, she receives but a scanty remuneration.

He closes against her all the avenues to wealth and distinction, which he considers most honorable to himself. As a teacher of theology, medicine, or law, she is not known.

He has denied her the facilities for obtaining a thorough education—all colleges being closed against her.

He allows her in Church as well as State, but a subordinate position, claiming Apostolic authority for her exclusion from the ministry, and, with some exceptions, from any public participation in the affairs of the Church.

He has created a false public sentiment by giving to the world a different code of morals for men and women, by which moral delinquencies which exclude women from society, are not only tolerated, but deemed of little account in man.

He has usurped the prerogative of Jehovah himself, claiming it as his right to assign for her a sphere of action, when that belongs to her conscience and to her God.

He has endeavored, in every way that he could, to destroy her confidence in her own powers, to lessen her self-respect, and to make her willing to lead a dependent and abject life.

Now, in view of this entire disfranchisement of one-half the people of this country, their social and religious degradation,—in view of the unjust laws above mentioned, and because women do feel themselves aggrieved, oppressed, and fraudulently deprived of their most sacred rights, we insist that they have immediate admission to all the rights and privileges which belong to them as citizens of these United States.

In entering upon the great work before us, we anticipate no small amount of misconception, misrepresentation, and ridicule; but we shall use every instrumentality within our power to effect our object. We shall employ agents, circulate tracts, petition the State and national Legislatures, and endeavor to enlist the pulpit and the press in our behalf. We hope this Convention will be followed by a series of Conventions, embracing every part of the country.

Firmly relying upon the final triumph of the Right and the True, we do this day affix our signatures to this declaration.

Index

A NOTE ON THE AUTHOR

Jean V. Matthews was born in London and studied at the University of London, Smith College, and Harvard University, where she received a Ph.D. in American history. She is the author of *Rufus Choate: The Law and Civic Virtue* and *Toward a New Society: American Thought and Culture, 1800–1830*. Ms. Matthews is professor emeritus at the University of Western Ontario and now lives in Oakland, California.